Pr...
The El...

C000076406

"This is a great representatio... ...g
the exchange-traded fund structure so many of us benefit
from today. It pays tribute to the people who were instrumental in innovating the ETF and pioneering the way with
regulators and industry participants. Thanks to them for
not giving up and to Ralph Lehman for sharing their story."

—Ronnee Ades
Executive, RAA Consulting; Master of Quantitative
Finance Program, Rutgers School of Business

"Throughout *The Elusive Trade*, Ralph Lehman chronicles
the nexus of the ETF as a trading solution in the wake of
1987's portfolio insurance disaster. Although the narrative
focuses on the ETF innovation as a trading solution, Mr.
Lehman also artfully transitions to the work of John Bogle
and Burton Malkiel, which evolved ETF adoption through
client alignment factors like lower cost, transparency, and
tax efficiency. Anyone interested in the birth of the ETF
industry or its evolution will enjoy *The Elusive Trade*."

—Mike Venuto
CIO, Toroso Investments

THE

ELUSIVE
TRADE

THE
ELUSIVE
TRADE

How Exchange-Traded Funds Conquered Wall Street

Ralph H. Lehman, CFA, CAIA, JD

BROWN BOOKS
PUBLISHING GROUP

The Elusive Trade
How Exchange-Traded Funds Conquered Wall Street

Brown Books Publishing Group
16250 Knoll Trail Drive, Suite 205
Dallas, Texas 75248
www.BrownBooks.com
(972) 381-0009

A New Era in Publishing®

Names: Lehman, Ralph H., author.
Title: The elusive trade : how exchange-traded funds conquered Wall
    Street / Ralph H. Lehman, CFA, CAIA, JD.
Description: Dallas, Texas : Brown Books Publishing Group, [2019] |
    Includes bibliographical references.
Identifiers: ISBN 9781612543079
Subjects: LCSH: Exchange traded funds. | Stock index futures.
Classification: LCC HG6043 .L44 2019 (print) | LCC HG6043 (ebook)
    | DDC 332.63/27--dc23

ISBN 978-1-61254-340-6 (PB)
LCCN 2018962444

Printed in the United States
10 9 8 7 6 5 4 3 2 1

For more information or to contact the author,
please go to www.TheElusiveTrade.com.

To my wife, Charlotte, who supported and encouraged me, and to the Lord, for His glory.

Contents

—— Acknowledgments ——

I am grateful to Foster Winans, who compressed and polished the lump of coal I provided him. Whether or not he created a diamond I will let the readers decide. Thanks so much to the team at Brown Books for their hard work, most notably Hallie, who labored over the myriad of citations and fine points of grammar; Earl and his design team; and Tom, who was willing to listen to an idea for a book from an untested author.

This book required input from scores of people who patiently related their experiences and insights. They have been dutifully credited in the endnotes of this book, but several of them deserve special credit. Barbara, Stephen, and Robert provided some fascinating and valuable insights into their father, Nate Most. Gary (go Cards!) and Todd shared their experiences of being on the Amex floor and trading the Spider. Kathleen walked me through the legal aspects of the Spider's approval around her constantly hectic schedule as she continues to be a vital part of the evolving ETF story. Hank opened my eyes to the critical work done that allowed the Spider and ETFs to trade. Kathy and Jim related the excellent work done by State Street for the Spider. Mac and Burton are two titans of finance who not only accepted my phone calls but went above and beyond in providing their insights and referrals. Fred guided me through the early days of indexing at WFIA. John and Hayne patiently related their innovative work with SuperTrust over several phone calls. Bill and Joseph walked me through the Philadelphia story. Andy was most helpful with the Canadian story and, like so many of the Canadians I interviewed, very understated and deflecting. Bob overwhelmed me with his insights into the ETF story, especially OPALS and WEBS, and was always available for the necessary follow-up phone calls as I tried to digest what he had provided (I still cannot decipher the patents awarded to this most creative man). Of these, Gary, Kathleen, Fred, Andy, Bob, and Joseph took special interest in this book and were a source of insight, encouragement, and, most importantly, referrals that allowed me to get the story straight.

I would also like to thank several people who are not in this book but were vital to it becoming a reality. First, Dave and the gang at ETF.com—some years ago I ventured to an Inside ETFs conference because I knew virtually nothing about ETFs. The rest, as they say, is history. A thanks to Perth, who introduced me to several people in the ETF community where the idea of this book originated, and to Arlene, the librarian of the ETF world, who jump-started my research by providing several key referrals and was a source of much-needed wisdom, encouragement, and humor throughout this process. To all of you who shared your time and insights into this wonderful story, thank you.

THE
ELUSIVE
TRADE

Introduction

The final quarter of the twentieth century saw an explosion of innovation in the financial markets with the introduction of new kinds of funds, strategies, and instruments. Terms that would have left our ancestors slack jawed became common lingo: hedge funds, private equity, derivatives, and collateralized debt obligations (CDOs)—the culprit behind the subprime mortgage crisis that spawned the Great Recession.

One of those new products that has not only endured but flourished is the exchange-traded fund (ETF). At the end of 2017, twenty-five years after ETFs first appeared, total assets in US-listed ETFs topped \$3.4 trillion,[1] roughly the same amount the federal government collects each year in taxes. This trend is set to continue. A 2017 investor survey by Charles Schwab found that more than four in ten ETF investors said ETFs "will be the primary investment vehicle in their portfolios in the future and 60% of Millennials expect to increase their investments in ETFs in the next year."[2]

As huge and attractive as the ETF market has become, few people understand what an ETF is. Fewer still know how an ETF operates, and just a handful can cite the history of the development of these securities, which have transformed the financial markets and the way people invest.

The short version is that exchange-traded funds emerged out of the wreckage of a previous market collapse, appearing first on stock exchanges that were in a fight for survival, marginalized by the confluence of consolidation and the technological revolution that was remaking Wall Street. The creation of ETFs resulted from a level of innovation that the financial community has rarely displayed—innovation that overwhelmingly benefitted investors as opposed to brokerage houses.

No other product has had such a transformative effect, involving contributions from some of Wall Street's most brilliant minds and a few unsung heroes. The ETF has stood on the shoulders of some of the giants in the financial industry and embodies a collection of many of the advances in portfolio management made in the post–World War II era, advances in less glamorous things such as trade execution and record keeping, and breakthroughs in finance technology.

One of the ironies of the growth in exchange-traded funds is that the physical exchanges we long associated with the financial markets are essentially extinct. The images of the floor of the New York Stock Exchange that accompany news reports about the markets are images of what is now practically a museum. Gone are the mobs of specialists in full-throated cry, waving scraps of paper and wading through drifts of ticker tape. Virtually all trading in financial vehicles now takes place in the silicon ether of technology.

One of the most common misconceptions about ETFs is that they trade like mutual funds. Both can be traded from any computer terminal, but, as the name implies, ETFs are traded on electronic exchanges. Mutual fund shares are bought directly from a mutual fund company. Both ETFs and mutual fund shares deal with the buying and selling of a portfolio of stocks, but the ETF is far more versatile. If a mutual fund is a pawn on the chessboard, an ETF is the queen.

The first ETFs appeared (in the US, as we shall see) in 1993 when the American Stock Exchange (the Amex), also on its way to extinction, launched a new type of security—Standard & Poor's depository receipts.[3] The SPDR fund—called the Spider—was the Amex's attempt to generate trading revenue to compensate for a steep decline in business. Unfortunately for the American Stock Exchange, the Spiders were thinly traded at first. The fund rose in popularity in 2003, and, except for a sharp pullback in 2011, the growth has been spectacular.

Twenty-five years after it first appeared, the SPDR is the largest ETF in the world, with more than $260 billion in assets under management and the most heavily traded securities on any exchange.[4]

Today's ETF was invented to facilitate a transaction that had been the holy grail of financial engineers: a single trade on a stock exchange that represented an entire portfolio. Until then, you could buy or sell a portfolio basket from a mutual fund company, but not on an exchange. On an exchange, you could sell all your holdings in a portfolio, but only in a closed-end fund, a cumbersome security that can suffer from poor liquidity and, hence, falling prices.

The solution to this conundrum has been refined since it was first introduced, but the basic structure that underlies most every ETF issued today traces its roots to the work done in the 1990s. Those who labored in obscurity and were not recognized until much later (some posthumously) were visionaries who, in some cases, took on enormous risks in the face of technological limitations, professional derision, fierce competition, and inept regulation.

My goal in these pages is to tell the story of the creation of the ETF: the academic research that laid the groundwork for index-based investing; the exchanges that were the first trading venues; the companies who refined the ETF structure. The principal characters in the story are a few of the people who led the way, believing that the ETF was a way of democratizing the markets by shifting power away from the large institutional program trading that had dominated security trading. As individual investors, we enjoy the fruits of their labors. My ambition is for this book to serve as a fitting tribute and a worthy addition to the rich history of our modern capital markets and the role they play in our lives.

1

When Money Met Machine

The saga of exchange-traded funds begins not on an exchange but at a bank—Wells Fargo, one of the oldest US banks still operating. Founded before the Civil War, Wells Fargo was born of the California Gold Rush. Before the transcontinental railroad connected our coasts, Wells Fargo wagons—the ones that still illustrate its corporate identity—carried communications into an otherwise isolated American West and shipped gold back east.[1] Aside from their forays into delivery, Wells Fargo operated much like a typical bank with traditional lines of business, managing client money in much the same way.

In the 1950s—a century after the firm was founded—this meant investing in grade-A bonds and select blue-chip stocks. A typical client might have owned just a dozen or so stocks of nationally recognized industrial and financial giants, perhaps with a smattering of smaller companies that were regional market leaders.

Active management prevailed throughout the investment industry. The few indexes that had appeared decades earlier were little more than financial mile markers. Charles Dow, cofounder of Dow Jones, introduced his Industrial Average of thirty stocks in the 1880s.[2] After a number of modifications, Standard & Poor's 500 Index assumed its present form in 1957.[3] These were useful tools in gauging the performance of the market and the health of the economy, but no one had yet entertained the notion of managing money by buying every stock in the index.

The prevailing wisdom was that it took a sharp investment advisor to select the stocks that would collectively beat the market. Investment as a field of research was in its infancy in the 1950s, and academic studies on it were sparse. The big bang came in 1955, except few people heard it. That was the year that the father of modern portfolio theory, economist Harry M. Markowitz, published his doctoral thesis, introducing the idea that by aggregating mathematical data about past stock performance, one could assemble a portfolio that would produce the best return for a given level of risk.[4] His work mostly gathered dust until the 1960s, when it began to attract other academics who built on his research. Wall Street then began to experiment with strategies and products that seemed to confirm his diversification approach, but it would be another quarter century before Markowitz received full credit for what proved to be a revolution in investment practices. In 1990, he was awarded the Nobel Prize in Economic Sciences.

Though it took a while for broad diversification to gain a foothold in the market, in the 1960s, Wells Fargo began to morph from pedestrian to avant-garde, eventually sponsoring much of the research that pushed the boundaries of portfolio management into frontier territory. The origins of this metamorphosis can be traced back to a single individual.

In the early 1960s, Ransom Cook, the chairman of Wells Fargo, attended a forum sponsored by IBM at which a man named John "Mac" McQuown, an analyst with Smith Barney & Co., talked about using computers to pick stocks.[5] McQuown had become intrigued with transistors and early computers while an engineering student at Northwestern University in Chicago. But he also immersed himself in the statistical analysis of investment strategies that continued at Markowitz's alma mater thirty miles down the Lake Michigan coast at the University of Chicago through friends he made with several graduate students in the Booth School of Business. McQuown had remained vigilant about keeping abreast of the subsequent discoveries advancing investment management even after he left Northwestern.

At Harvard Business School, McQuown had combined his twin interests in computers and stocks. At IBM's forum, he was a compelling advocate for the need for computers to pick stocks in this new, well-funded market. After his address, Cook offered McQuown a job on the spot.

For the next decade, McQuown was director of the Management Sciences Group (MSG), a think tank within Wells Fargo that reported directly to the CEO. McQuown became the founder and first chair of the bank's investment advisory subsidiary, Wells Fargo Investment Advisors (WFIA). Under his stewardship, the bank worked with a who's who of financial innovators, including Markowitz. The research that was generated undermined the argument for active management—stock picking—in favor of passive (index) investing. Wells Fargo's trust and investment divisions were slow to embrace the work coming out of McQuown's group, but they eventually came on board. WFIA went on to play a singularly pivotal role in the development of exchange-traded funds.

The first index portfolio at Wells Fargo Investment Advisors was funded by Samsonite, the luggage company, to manage the firm's $6 million in pension assets.[6] McQuown's group developed the software, and WFIA managed the day-to-day operations. William Fouse, whom McQuown had recruited from Mellon Bank, was the lead manager for launching the vision. WFIA set out to track the fifteen hundred stocks trading on the New York Stock Exchange (NYSE) in 1971.[7]

What seemed straightforward in theory proved arduous and cumbersome in practice. The computers available for use in trading operations weren't robust enough to handle simultaneous transactions in the fifteen hundred securities while trying to maintain targeted equal weighting among them throughout each day's session. But technology continued to improve, and WFIA refined their approach, scaling back the scope of the project by choosing a less ambitious index, the S&P 500, made up of the most liquid stocks.

The seed money for the project included pension funds from Wells Fargo and Illinois Bell Telephone. The Samsonite pension funds later folded into the commingled account.[8] The intersection of sophisticated financial innovation meeting the needs of often-forgotten individual investors is a theme found throughout the ETF story. But academics and innovators also understood where the assets lay, and pensions provided the largest pools they could use to put their theories into practice. The first beneficiaries of Wells Fargo's market innovations were middle-class families saving for retirement, an example of the market democratization that would be characteristic of the exchange-traded funds traded later. During McQuown's tenure at Wells Fargo, his group also launched a passively managed low-beta (low-volatility) fund that would be leveraged to enhance the return.[9] It was designed by two of investment history's brightest stars: Fischer Black, a Harvard-educated applied mathematics expert who was a pioneer in artificial intelligence, and Myron Scholes, another Chicago school of economics alumnus. In the 1960s, they had collaborated on developing a mathematical pricing formula—the Black-Scholes model—that became to our understanding of the financial world what Einstein's $E = mc^2$ became to our understanding of the physical world. Scholes would go on to win the 1997 Nobel Prize for his work on derivatives.

The fund that resulted from their collaboration embodied much of what would be recognized as innovation in the ETF industry three decades later. Black wanted to address the penalty paid by investors who were undercompensated for holding high-beta stocks.[10] Although Fouse argued that such a strategy would overweight certain industries, such as banking and finance, with McQuown's blessing, the plan moved forward.

For two years, the innovative, commingled Stagecoach fund was offered to the bank's institutional clients. Then First National City Bank (now Citibank) began marketing a similar product. The appearance of these first passively managed funds was, in the eyes of most, utter heresy. Since the 1930s, fund management had been the exclusive province of brokerage firms and mutual fund companies, not computers.

The question of whether to keep it that way became the subject of public debate beginning in the early 1960s.[11] In

1966, the US Comptroller of Currency and the US Securities and Exchange Commission (SEC) granted National City Bank an exemption from the rule—and the fight was on.[12] In 1970, the Investment Company Institute (ICI), the mutual fund's trade association, filed a petition in federal court challenging the exemption, which allowed banks to offer commingled investment funds like the ones that had been developed at Wells Fargo and National City. The case ended up in front of the Supreme Court, which, ruling 6–2 for the mutual fund industry, described the case as "a double barreled assault upon the efforts of a national bank to go into the business of operating a mutual investment fund."[13]

Wells Fargo could not offer its exchange-traded fund to retail customers, but it could continue to offer it to institutional investors. The mutual fund industry had beaten back a viable threat, but it had, for the most part, completely missed the opportunity that was the substance of that threat. John C. Bogle, a mutual fund executive, knew it. He launched an index fund tied to the S&P 500 and named it Vanguard after a famous British warship. Beginning with just $11 million in assets under management, Vanguard today manages in excess of $5 trillion, and Bogle is universally recognized as one of the greatest financial custodians of the twentieth century.

But McQuown, frustrated by the mutual fund industry's stubborn resistance to the wave of the future and finding the bank's horizons too limited, left Wells Fargo. In 1981, he cofounded an investment company called Dimensional Fund Advisors (DFA) with two graduates of UCBSB (University of Chicago Booth School of Business) classmates of his, David Booth and Rex Sinquefield.[14] The principles developed for Wells Fargo's Stagecoach fund were refined and applied at DFA to a full suite of funds. Today, DFA manages nearly $600 billion. As a result of the mutual fund industry's myopic zeal in thwarting competition, it passed up close to $6 trillion in ETF assets.

Wells Fargo, meanwhile, continued its commitment to indexing. Fouse, the executive whom McQuown had lured away from Mellon, remained at Wells Fargo and developed a strategy that applied indexing to multiple asset classes—stocks, bonds, and cash—as opposed to just stock indexes. As expected returns in each class rose or fell, the allocation among the classes was adjusted up or down. This became known as tactical asset allocation (TAA). Portfolios were rebalanced annually based on a set of metrics, the goal being to create a vehicle managed passively (as opposed to actively).

Detractors argued that tactical asset allocation was nothing more than market timing, a gimmick to sneak active management in through the back door. But the proof was in the pudding: from 1977 until 2000, TAA proved to be the best performing manager of all, outperforming even the venerable Warren Buffett without leverage or hedging, two tools active that managers often employ to boost their results but that come at the cost of additional risk.[15] For his roles in both indexing and TAA, Fouse was later hailed by some financial journalists, one of whom referred to him as "the greatest investor you've never heard of."[16]

Wells Fargo Investment Advisors remained a recognized leader throughout much of the 1970s. But without McQuown at the helm, the firm developed internal problems and began to flounder. The bank began searching for another visionary. Most of the firms from which Wells Fargo would be expected to poach new leadership were still committed to active management. The passive-investing model was new enough that it was hard to get clients excited about breaking with tradition, and the prevailing instinct was to avoid fixing what wasn't broken. WFIA turned to its network of academic advisors, most of whom traced their lineage to the University of Chicago.

Wells Fargo eventually chose Frederick L. A. Grauer as the new head of WFIA. Grauer was a Canadian who had earned his master of economics degree at the University of Chicago and his doctorate in business at Stanford University. As if those credentials weren't enough, Grauer had studied under a half dozen or more of the leading lights in the study of economics. Grauer was a teaching professor at Columbia University, and his orbit did not extend beyond academia until the Chicago Mercantile Exchange

(CME) and the Commodity Exchange (COMEX)—the two primary exchanges for futures contracts—agreed to fund a study of the futures market.[17] Futures contracts—agreements between two parties for the delivery of some asset (wheat, corn, pork bellies, gold, currency, etc.) at some specified future date at a predetermined price—have been around since the early 1600s and have been in the US since the Civil War, structured to hedge against volatile commodities prices. The first financial futures contracts were created in 1972 by the International Monetary Market, a spin-off from the Chicago Mercantile Exchange.[18]

Grauer was recruited to take the helm at Wells Fargo Investment Advisors in 1979, but the match didn't take.[19] He left after only eighteen months, explaining, "I couldn't stop being an academic, pointing out things I saw that were wrong."[20] He landed at Merrill Lynch, where he spent three years wooing institutional clients (the firm's nickname was Merrill Lunch) and discovering that he found the hustle and bustle of commerce more appealing than the hush of academia. He learned the art of nurturing clients and managing people. Like McQuown, at Merrill Lynch he showed a knack for finding ways to connect people with diverse agendas and styles.

But without someone to lead it into the future, by 1983, Wells Fargo was "on the brink of collapse," and its top executives were abandoning ship.[21] William Fouse left to return to his previous employer, Mellon, where he set up Mellon Capital Management. In a kind of financial musical chairs, Grauer was recruited from Merrill to head up the rescue mission, and he, too, returned to his previous employer.

Upon his return to Wells Fargo, Grauer hit the ground running—and nurturing. He insisted on interviewing job candidates himself, looking for people who fit his diverse-culture sensibility and who were fired up and ready to go.[22] Under Grauer, WFIA grew exponentially, spreading into new lines of business that could take advantage of indexing and passive investing. The focus was on institutional clients and pensions, especially outside of the US, where the concepts and tactics he and others were bringing to portfolio management remained a hard sell. One market that turned out to be underdeveloped—and therefore fertile territory—was Japan. Entry for foreign firms required a domestic partner, so in 1990, Grauer negotiated the sale of half of the firm to Nikko Securities.[23] The combination quickly became the second-largest asset manager in Japan. Five years later, in a move that would prove to be a case of terrible timing, Wells Fargo decided to sell off its Investment Advisors business—just as the ETF market was about to take off.[24] Wells Fargo Bank would no longer be part of the ETF story, but its progeny would continue to be a driving force.

2

The ETF Spark

When the silicon chip came on the scene, it completely rewrote the rules of trading and investing. Early iterations of computers had made it possible for academics to crunch vast amounts of data to test indexing concepts and produce portfolio models. Wells Fargo, Vanguard, and Dimensional Fund Advisors were enthusiastic early adopters of the technology, but the industry hesitated to follow, in part because trading volume was beginning to outstrip the exchanges' ability to manage it. A major issue arose in 1968 when the New York Stock Exchange declared a "paperwork crisis" and, for several months, suspended trading on Wednesdays to give firms time to catch up.[1] "Fails"—firms' inability to receive or deliver physical stock certificates to execute and close out transactions—soared. By some estimates, as many as one hundred smaller, undercapitalized brokerages went under.

Amid the voluminous paperwork, counterfeit certificates for AT&T, GE, Chrysler, and other blue chips began showing up at the NYSE.[2] Attorney General John Mitchell told a Senate investigations subcommittee that, during 1969 and 1970, close to $500 million worth of securities ($3 billion after inflation) had been stolen by organized crime syndicates. An editorial in the *New York Times* suggested, "Probably the most effective way to reduce the volume of lost and stolen securities would be to eliminate the traditional stock certificate."[3, 4]

By the 1980s, technological issues had essentially solved the paper problem, but they made possible the next one: the digital crisis. The National Security Clearing Corporation and the Depository Trust Company improved security trading by enabling faster execution while also increasing reliability.

Smaller regional exchanges led the way into computerized trading. Previously, computers had been employed to deliver trades to an exchange and then to execute some of the trades at the exchange. Then the Cincinnati Stock Exchange became the nation's first all-electronic trading market in 1976, albeit for only forty stocks.[5, 6] As the major exchanges adapted to paperless systems and instant price quotes, brokers and exchanges alike began exploring how to trade larger baskets of stocks, but these strategies remained the domain of institutional clients, not retail ones.

For individual investors, buying and selling all the stocks in a diversified portfolio proved to be too clumsy and costly. Brokerage commissions were only beginning to come down. They could, however, purchase a basket of stocks through shares in a mutual fund, also known as an open-end fund. This had its own drawback: open-end funds did not trade on any exchange. Smaller investors had to purchase shares directly from the mutual fund company. Mutual fund companies held their buy and sell orders until after the exchanges closed at 4:00 p.m., at which time these consolidated trades received the final price of each stock, thus providing the fund's share price as well as its net asset value.

The second basketlike vehicle available to individual investors at the time was known as a closed-end mutual fund. Formed through an initial public offering, these could issue a fixed number of shares and no more. These shares possessed the advantage of trading throughout the day on an exchange floor, but the fund's price as listed on the exchange usually deviated from the net asset value per share of the investments held by the fund. Because this additional risk could not be effectively hedged, investors never fully embraced closed-end funds. At the end of 2017, the total assets of closed-end funds were $275 billion, versus nearly $19 trillion held by mutual funds.[7, 8]

Brokers, exchanges, and investors all had a compelling interest in the ability to sell a portfolio in a single trade. The reduced transaction costs and simplicity appealed to investors. Brokers and traders could employ strategies that would otherwise be cost prohibitive or impossible to execute. And exchanges—especially those not named the New York Stock Exchange—were interested in any new securities that could be traded on their floors, especially if the securities comprising that basket would otherwise trade on the Big Board.

The twin forces of research and innovation were reshaping markets and investments in a myriad of ways. The intersection of those forces struck the spark that would result in the creation of ETFs. Until the enabling technology came along, the notion of trading an entire portfolio was wishful thinking—a riddle that was a source of frustration. This was never more evident than on Black Monday.

3

Black Monday

Ask any trader, broker, portfolio manager, or investor who was actively engaged in the world of finance whether they remember where they were on October 19, 1987. They will likely be able to tell you with the same specificity that members of other generations would use to describe where they were when President John F. Kennedy was shot or Pearl Harbor was bombed. On the day dubbed Black Monday, the Dow Jones Industrial Average cratered, plunging by 508 points—nearly a quarter of the aggregate market value.[1] Comparisons were immediately made to the Great Crash of October 1929, which began on a day that came to be known as Black Thursday and continued on the following Black Monday and Black Tuesday. Adjusted for inflation, that collapse was a bloodbath of more than $400 billion, which doesn't sound so bad until you consider that much of it was so leveraged and unhedged that fortunes in paper wealth were wiped out overnight. Black Thursday was when window jumping became synonymous with a bad day on Wall Street.

Fears of a second Great Depression failed to materialize in 1987. A short, shallow recession came two years later. Over the next five years, the market clawed its way back to its precrash level, and then the markets took off, setting record after record before topping out just before the big internet crash started in 2000. There was no window jumping, but Black Monday did serve as a catalyst for profound changes in the markets, especially in how securities were bought and sold. It exposed critical deficiencies in the functioning of the stock market. Some of the malfunction could be traced back to things as basic as Nasdaq market makers refusing to answer their phones, making it impossible for customers to initiate trades. But it was computers that brought the financial world to its knees on Black Monday, a day that proved to be the beginning of the end for traditional exchange trading.

Of course, the meaning of "traditional trading" had changed somewhat over the last century with the adoption of new technologies such as ticker tape and the telephone. Each local exchange had a niche in which they could operate without much direct competition. But the rate of change had sped up, altering exchanges at their very core.

The New York Stock Exchange, confronted by shrinking margins, was finding it necessary to become more aggressive. The Nasdaq was asserting itself and proving to be a formidable competitor. Companies were beginning to reject the overtures of other stock exchanges and choosing to remain with the Nasdaq. The American Stock Exchange, long the nation's second-largest exchange, was struggling just to stay open while being squeezed by both the New York Stock Exchange and the Nasdaq.

The Amex was an *auction market*—buyers and sellers would come together and make their bids and offers on the exchange floor. The New York Stock Exchange was a *dealer market*—multiple brokers listed the prices of the securities they bought and sold. Auction markets typically operated smoothly but would occasionally become unbalanced between buyers and sellers. Certain brokers, called specialists, would then step in and restore order. Specialists used their own capital to purchase shares when the market had more sellers than buyers and, when necessary, sold shares from their inventory. This system had served the Amex well in the past, but like the exchanges, the specialist model was facing disruptions in an age of computer efficiency, greater transparency, and the increased flow of information between exchanges.

Black Monday hit all players of the old order hard. One culprit that many held responsible for all the mayhem turned out to be a popular hedging technique—a bit of financial engineering called portfolio insurance, which investment managers thought protected them from a sudden market downdraft. It didn't, in part because program trading, as the tactic was called then, was so widespread. It was as if half of all the cars on the road all had accidents at the same time and all filed claims on the same day. On Black Monday, the flood of sell orders so swamped the New York Stock Exchange that trading had to be halted in stock after stock. The Chicago Mercantile Exchange threatened to halt trading in stock index futures. With trading suspended in so many stocks, it was impossible to calculate the actual value of a stock index. The Associated Press—which, every trading day, reported the closing stock tables starting when the markets closed at 4:00 p.m.—didn't even begin sending data until 9:30 that night.

The volume generated by the Black Monday collapse so overwhelmed the Nasdaq's trading system that, like an overloaded circuit breaker, it repeatedly shut down over the course of the session.[2]

Black Monday tested the various markets and exposed their weaknesses. Stock exchanges, futures exchanges, and options exchanges all suffered breakdowns to some extent during that tumultuous Monday. The technology that had been increasing the trading volume on the exchanges now unleashed a fury of trades that none of the markets or exchanges could keep pace with. The flow of information between exchanges, a hallmark of progress, became proof that the old must give way to the new.

The digital crisis was on. A quarter of a century later, Floyd Norris, at the time a reporter for *Barron's*, recalled, "It was the beginning of the destruction of markets by dumb computers. Or, to be fair to the computers, by computers programmed by fallible people and trusted by people who did not understand the computer programs' limitations. As computers came in, human judgment went out."[3]

There were, however, a few bright spots. Just the Friday before, the Amex had installed a refinement to its computerized trading system that went live for the first time the day of the sell-off. In spite of one-day volume that was triple the usual volume of an entire month, the system worked.[4] The Amex desperately needed new business, and its performance under fire helped it steal a few listings away from the over-the-counter (OTC) market.[5]

Morgan Stanley Trust Company was another firm that had reason to pat itself on the back at the end of the day on October 19, 1987. The company had just sunk an inflation-adjusted quarter-billion dollars into building a state-of-the-art trading system from scratch. Many in the company had opposed the project. The price was staggeringly high because it was a big departure from the prevailing entry system, known as "corridor trade processing," which handled orders sequentially. It would not move on to the next trade until any errors in the current trade had been resolved. This required the operations staff to continually engage the system to clear glitches, such as an incorrect ticker symbol; a wrong

CUSIP (the nine-digit alphanumeric identifier for US securities); trades requiring more shares than an account held; a trade sent to the wrong exchange for execution; or trades for securities not yet set up in the system. With sixty thousand trades a day to process at Morgan Stanley, corridor execution was tedious, laborious, and demanded constant vigilance.

Instead, the firm's operations team developed a proprietary system called "wave processing."[6] Trades that required no intervention were stored for processing and then distributed to subcustodian banks and foreign brokers for batch settlement. Trades that needed editing went into a repair queue, where they were corrected and, time permitting, processed that trading day. The new system kept error-free trades from getting stuck in the pipeline and enabled the operations staff to correct errors affecting a group of trades (because, say, the CUSIP or ticker had changed) in one fell swoop instead of piecemeal.

The person spearheading the new system at Morgan Stanley was Robert Tull, whose résumé was something of an oddity at such a venerable, white-shoe, Ivy League firm. He had been a premed student in college, studying physics and chemistry, when he had to drop out due to lack of tuition. His father, a lifelong employee of the Pennsylvania Railroad, had invested virtually all of his savings in the company. In 1968, it merged with the New York Central

Railroad and became the Penn Central. Within two years, the new management had driven the merged systems into the ground, wiping out Tull's college fund. He landed at a commodities trading firm, where he learned, among other things, the trade-processing system. He made a lateral move to the commodity-trading desk at Morgan Stanley and was later tapped to oversee development of the trust's new trading system.

The project began in May 1987 with a target rollout date of November 1. The team completed the project several weeks ahead of schedule and, on October 17 and 18—the weekend before Black Monday—put the system through a series of rigorous tests.[7] Everything worked, and Tull left the office on Sunday night having decided to reward himself by taking off the next day.

On a mild, damp fall morning—Black Monday—Tull set his phone to send all calls to his answering machine and threw himself into an unfinished landscaping project. He finally got around to checking his messages in the afternoon and found the tape full of tense, frightened voices describing some sort of financial apocalypse. He grabbed his "go bag"—standard equipment for Morgan personnel, containing everything necessary for an emergency business trip—and raced into the office to find that the new trading system had functioned without a hitch. Morgan Stanley was one of the few firms to successfully process all of its

Black Monday trades, including those of its largest client, Wells Fargo Investment Advisors. That night, an executive with San Francisco–based discount broker Charles Schwab & Co. called, frantically looking to be rescued after its trading system crashed.

What had, twenty-four hours earlier, looked to some like a high-risk gamble with no clear payback was now a genius move, and Robert Tull was now a star.

Black Monday changed the game for stock markets in general; specifically, it wreaked havoc on options traders. An option is a security that gives the holder the right to buy or sell another security at a set price within a set period of time—typically less than a year, more commonly a few months. For example, a call (to buy) option for Microsoft with a strike price of $120 gives the option buyer the right to purchase Microsoft stock at $120 before the option expires. If the stock fails to trade at $120 or better, the option expires, worthless. If the stock has risen above $120 at any time before expiration, the price of the option will probably have gone up, and the holder could buy the stock at the lower price or sell the option at a profit, which is what usually happens.

The same mechanism applies to put options, but they give the holder the right to sell a stock at a certain price by a certain time. A portfolio manager holding a large, long-term position in a stock such as Microsoft may be vulnerable to a bear market. As stocks decline, investment managers may be forced to sell some of their holdings to raise cash as a defensive measure, even though they are confident the company is still a good investment. Instead, the common practice is to invest in put options that ordinarily rise in value as the underlying stock falls. The manager books a profit on the options, which helps offset the paper loss without actually have to sell any shares.

Black Monday wrecked a lot of traders, investment managers, and investors, but it boosted the careers of a few visionaries whose work was laying the foundation for today's ETFs. One of those was Thomas J. Dorsey, cofounder of Dorsey Wright & Associates, a technology-driven financial data-crunching consultancy. He is known, among other things, for Dorsey Wright's point and figure methodology, a popular system for tracking volatility in the price of any actively traded asset. You may have seen the distinctive charts based on the Dorsey Wright method portraying price movements as vertical rows of Xs and Os. The method was developed to take emotion and guesswork out of picking the best times to buy or sell.

Like Morgan Stanley's Robert Tull, Dorsey's college career had been cut short, in his case by undiagnosed dyslexia. Also like Tull, Dorsey was blessed with exquisite timing. In January 1987, Dorsey and Watson Wright, a colleague he had worked with at regional brokerage firm

Wheat First Securities, went into business together developing options strategies aimed at producing above-market returns.[8]

Dorsey had been an early options adopter when he began his career at Merrill Lynch in 1974, halfway through the longest muddle in stock market history. In 1966, the Dow Jones Industrial Average had hit a peak of just under 1,000. It would be sixteen years, in October 1982, before the index finally broke above that raw number and nearly three decades before it bested the 1966 peak on an inflation-adjusted basis.[9]

As a new broker learning the ropes, Dorsey overheard phone calls from disillusioned and exasperated clients demanding to their brokers, "Send me what is left in my account, and don't call me back!" He realized that he would need to come up with something that would set him apart during a time when far more brokers were leaving the industry than entering. He made a quote by Ralph Waldo Emerson his mantra: "Make yourself necessary to somebody."

Dorsey kept his eye out for a fresh idea that the older, more established brokers would be unfamiliar with. His search brought him to financial options, which had debuted the previous year on the Chicago Board Options Exchange (CBOE) and which the Philadelphia Exchange (PHLX) was now offering. He set out to become the go-to guy on options at Merrill Lynch.

Options might have been new to the modern financial markets at the time, but they had been around since ancient history in the form of contracts between parties to facilitate trade in commodities that took a long time to travel between payment and delivery and were at risk of robbery and disaster. Early options were quirky and fraught with counterparty risks and illiquidity. By standardizing options elements, removing counterparty risk, and providing a centralized trading location, the CBOE vastly increased liquidity and made options strategies viable. Dorsey was determined to learn everything he could about the new type of security type, but no existing model seemed to work as a price-tracking mechanism. There were no computers yet, and handheld calculators had only just been introduced. Still, Dorsey surmounted these challenges, and it didn't take long for the young broker to become Merrill's expert on all things options.

By January 1987, Dorsey was an options guru, and when he and Wright founded their company and began marketing their proprietary strategies, he was the right person in the right place at the right time. The Tax Reform Act of 1986, a major initiative to simplify the tax code and eliminate many tax shelters, had just gone into effect. Anticipation of the impact of these changes was driving the market higher at a dizzying pace. Between September 1985 and August 1987—less than two months before Black Monday—the

Dow Jones Average had more than doubled.[10] Dorsey was convinced that his charts were signaling a sell-off.[11]

After hitting an all-time high on August 25, the market began retreating.[12] In early October, the Dow meandered for a week or so—a little up, a little down—within about eighty points of twenty-five hundred, as if trying to decide which way to go next. Because the markets had been on such a tear, some well-followed analysts had been warning about a pullback. That fed into a curious Wall Street superstition born of two historic crashes in stock market history—1907 and 1929. Both had taken place in October. (As of 2018, half of the top ten largest one-day percentage declines in the history of the Dow struck in October.) Although prices have historically gone up more than down in October, when the Halloween decorations go up there's always hand wringing about a possible "October surprise."[13]

On Wednesday, October 14, 1987, the markets were especially jittery. All the indexes finished in the red. The Dow sank 4 percent—a sizeable swing, but not, by itself, enough to sow panic. But on Thursday, the weakness continued. Then a massive North Atlantic storm system with hurricane-force winds plunged much of London into a blackout, halting trading on the London Stock Exchange. Friday brought wild price swings and the most shares ever traded on the Big Board in a single day. It was the first time the Dow had ever closed down by one hundred points in a single session.

That afternoon, before the closing bell, Dorsey had a hunch that bottom-fishing traders who had been on the sidelines watching prices get punished would be looking to reenter the market on Monday's opening. He bet that they would be counting on a short-term rebound—what traders refer to as a "dead cat bounce." Short sellers who wanted to cover their positions and lock in profits would normally be in the market buying first thing Monday morning, giving prices a temporary boost. Like a dead cat, there would be only one spike before the sell-off resumed.

Dorsey directed his firm to buy ten call option contracts on the S&P 100, which traded under the OEX ticker. The index had fallen by 30 percent in four days, so the options were trading at a discount, signaling a down opening on Monday that Dorsey was betting against. Instead, Monday began a bloodbath that broke all the records—twice Friday's record volume. The Dow plunged 220 points in the final hour of trading to close with a one-day record decline of 22 percent—508 points.[14]

But Dorsey got his own October surprise: the options rose in value, seeming to defy financial gravity. What had happened?

The principal factor determining an option's value is the sum of the market capitalization of all the underlying assets. In the case of the S&P 100—OEX—it's the hundred large companies that make up the index. What Dorsey discovered is that the volatility of those asset prices was equally important. The more volatility, the better the chance the index will rebound from a steep decline, and vice versa. While the market was tanking, Dorsey's OEX options had doubled in price. But the market soon stabilized, and the option price fell before Dorsey Wright could get out with a profit. Dorsey learned two important lessons from Black Monday. The first was the importance of volatility in options. The second was that options would never recapture the favor they had enjoyed up until Black Monday. The firm needed a new strategy. Drawing on their expertise in charting, the firm decided to focus on technical analysis.

Later analysis of what happened on Black Friday found that most traders were convinced, at various points during the day, that prices had fallen as far as they reasonably could . . . but they hadn't. Stocks of blue chips like IBM shed a third of their value while nothing fundamental had changed for the company. Traders filled with confidence stopped hedging their positions and began writing naked (unhedged) call options that were deep out of the money, meaning the traders would be on the hook if the positions didn't pan out. The markets rebounded quickly, posting record gains on both Tuesday and Thursday of the same week. But the options markets did not. The rebound left many traders in the hole.[15]

Many option traders, like Dorsey, survived the carnage of Black Monday, but others were less fortunate. More than a hundred smaller trading firms were wiped. Stock investors could hold their investments and see how the market would play out. Not so for those on the wrong side of an option. If they were unable to deliver, they were cashiered from trading.

After the crash, the options market continued to expand, as they were written on an increasing number of securities. But the only portfolio baskets available for options were illiquid indexes. This curtailed the investing and hedging strategies many sought. Like the stock market, options suffered from the lack of a portfolio trade. The options market had failed a crucial test, but failure is always the planting ground of innovation.

4

Portfolio Uncertainty

Black Monday turned the options industry upside down, but options escaped blame for precipitating the crash. Such was not the case for an investment strategy involving stock futures. In January 1988, *Fortune* reported, "A prime topic of conversation, especially among people eager to fix blame for the day the Dow lost 508 points . . . has focused on Hayne Leland, John O'Brien, and Mark Rubinstein, the inventors and evangelists of portfolio insurance . . . that many think made the plunge steeper and deeper than it would have been otherwise."[1]

Only three years earlier, Leland, O'Brien, and Rubinstein had founded a firm to offer a revolutionary product designed to protect portfolios against large losses to pension funds and institutional clients. In the same way that Wells Fargo had pioneered much of the work in index investing, Leland, O'Brien, and Rubinstein (LOR) would do much of the groundbreaking work for exchange-traded funds. But first, the firm had to cope with the black eye it had gotten for its role in exacerbating the damage on Black Monday.

Hayne Leland had followed his older brother into the investment business. Leland was intrigued by the connections between economics and the stock market. He earned his bachelor's degree and doctorate from Harvard and his master's from the London School of Economics. At a family gathering, Leland's brother, John, an investment manager for Rosenberg Capital Insurance, talked about the bear market of 1973–74, where the Dow plunged nearly 40 percent, and how it was made worse because many institutional managers sat on their hands as prices plunged instead of buying solid stocks at a discount. Hayne's brother lamented, "It's too bad that they could not have bought some insurance and stayed active in the market."[2]

Hayne Leland, who had become an economics professor at the University of California, Berkeley, was intrigued by the idea of designing a vehicle with similar characteristics to put options that had first been introduced on the CBOE in 1973. Drawing on the Black-Scholes options pricing model—a mathematical equation for creating a call option or "synthetic stock"—Leland designed a synthetic put that contemplated selling stock in a portfolio as the market fell and buying back into the market as it rebounded. In retrospect, it was an obvious strategy, but at the time, it was novel.

In 1979, Hayne began collaborating with Mark Rubinstein, a colleague at Berkeley who had published research on options pricing.[3] Rubinstein and his colleagues had developed an option-trading strategy that they tested on the Pacific Stock Exchange, one of four exchanges that had received approval to trade such experimental securities. The strategy earned a profit, although, in the end, they lost most of it due to inexperience. But the experience convinced them they had found the key to something potentially huge.[4] Leland and Rubinstein formed a partnership and set about refining their idea and pitching it to major banks, including Wells Fargo and Morgan Guaranty. Living on their teaching salaries, Leland and Rubinstein lacked the capital to market their ideas broadly and were unable to land their first client.

Then they met John O'Brien, a risk analyst with A. G. Becker, a century-old investment bank based in Chicago that was in the final throes of an ownership battle with Merrill Lynch. O'Brien had earned degrees in engineering and economics at MIT before spending four years in the Air Force, where he had worked in war gaming, making risk assessments. He heard a pitch by Leland and Rubinstein and tried to get A. G. Becker to sign up, but the firm wasn't interested.[5] So O'Brien left Becker, and Leland O'Brien Rubinstein (LOR) was born.

O'Brien had persuasion skills and contacts his partners lacked, so he took up the position of CEO and primary salesman. LOR slowly accumulated assets to manage until

1983, when futures for the major market indexes began trading and the business began to boom. Instead of selling stocks in a down market, they could sell futures on the S&P 500 Index and hold on to their positions. This "portfolio insurance" was less expensive and easier to implement. Johns Manville Corp.'s pension fund, Wells Fargo, and Aetna Insurance became marquee clients. At its peak, the firm managed about $150 billion, adjusted for inflation.[6] And then Black Monday hit.

The strategy that LOR had developed—using computer systems to manage large-scale trades—was easily replicated and had been widely copied. But the capability to place thousands of orders during a crash had never been tested. Stocks plunged to stop-loss levels, triggering sell orders, but the same programs automatically turned off all buy orders. Without buyers, the prices kept ratcheting down, triggering additional orders. Bids vanished, and the bottom dropped out.

LOR sold about one-third of the futures that their algorithm was telling them to sell during Black Monday.[7] Their models had led them to believe they could sell enough futures to insulate their investors from the market's fury, but their model did not take into account how ubiquitous the strategy had become and how frenzied the futures market could become. Although the strategy had come up short, it did effectively mitigate losses for some clients. A portfolio manager at Kidder Peabody told the *LA Times*, "I was responding to the LOR insurance strategy when I went fully liquid and converted to money markets on Friday, and I stayed whole."[8] A Merrill Lynch manager told the paper that LOR's program helped stem losses in one insured portfolio, leaving $230 million in equity intact.[9] But those were by the far the exceptions.

So many other institutions had adopted LOR's insurance strategy that when they all threw in the towel at the same time, attempting to sell their stocks to nonexistent buyers, a bloodbath ensued. Before Black Friday, LOR CEO O'Brien's problem had been persuading the investment community to take the firm's esoteric strategy seriously. After Black Monday, the firm found itself at the center of a raging controversy over its role in causing the worst crash in history. The partners were taking so much fire that they refused to allow their photos to be taken because it might be dangerous.

In spite of all of it, in spite of losing some of their big accounts, LOR survived Black Monday. On Tuesday, Leland, O'Brien, and Rubinstein set about working on a new idea, one that was not dependent upon the futures market, which, like the stock and options markets, had come up short.[10]

Two Reports

Black Monday, 1987, joined a roster of major market break-downs stretching back more than a century. The Panic of 1873 started in Europe but metastasized in the US when Jay Cooke & Co., America's first national wire house and the biggest marketer of US bonds during the Civil War, went bankrupt overextending itself while trying to construct the second transcontinental railroad.[1] The railroad industry was rife with overvalued and undercapitalized companies, many of which also went bankrupt. The six years that followed the Panic of 1873 would come to be known as the Great Depression until that depression was dwarfed half a century later.

The San Francisco earthquake was the backdrop for the next crash. The earthquake drained a lot of liquidity from the financial system. This crash proved to be another October surprise and was dubbed the 1907 Bankers' Panic. Triggered by a failed attempt to corner the stock of United Copper Company and the subsequent failure of the Knickerbocker Trust, the Panic of 1907 cut the capitalization of the NYSE in half. For the first time, Congress responded by establishing the Federal Reserve in 1913 to provide support for the markets in times of crisis. This set a precedent for the governmental response to the famed Stock Market Crash of 1929, when the Senate Banking and Currency Committee's investigation into market mismanagement produced a blizzard of legislation: the Securities Act of 1933; the Securities and Exchange Act of 1934; and, much later, the Investment Advisers Act of 1940.[2]

Although Black Monday inspired no such regulatory fever, President Reagan did establish the Presidential Task Force on Market Mechanisms, whose findings became known as the Brady Report after its chair, Nicholas Brady.[3] An investment banker and former senator from New Jersey, Brady was appointed secretary of the Treasury soon after the report was issued.

The Brady Report cited program trading and portfolio insurance as contributors to the crash, but it placed more of the blame on aggressive selling by a few large institutions that so dominated the markets that they were able to get their trades executed early in the session. More than six hundred million shares traded hands on the New York Stock Exchange that Monday, nearly double the record established by the previous session on Friday.[4] The numbers defied imagination.

The technology of trading was still a work in progress, favoring institutions over retail investors. Individual investors placed trades over phones with their brokers—if they were able to get through and if the broker was inclined to pick up the receiver. Institutional investors had their trades placed electronically, sent directly to the exchange floors for execution.[5]

A second inequality had to do with the popularity of mutual funds among retail investors. On Black Monday, as on every other day, mutual fund trades were executed after the close. These included orders placed late in the afternoon of the preceding session, Friday. Mutual fund holders with pending sell orders were at the mercy of the market, which trimmed 20 percent off of what some holders had hoped to receive.

Retail investors who had some money to put to work and had decided that the smart thing to do was to buy mutual fund shares the next day experienced the opposite. They watched in dismay as the market rallied, boosting the Dow by more than one hundred points, making their purchases much costlier than they had looked that morning. Like the vineyard workers in the biblical parable who were paid the same amount regardless of whether they worked all day or just the last hour, mutual fund investors received the same price for their shares regardless of whether they placed the order at the opening bell or at 3:00 p.m.

Although there was no call for regulation, the crash had to be explained. Once the dust had settled, the SEC went to work, producing its report on the October 1987 market break the following February. In the executive summary, the report's authors explained that the investigation was not aimed at answering "the question of why in October of 1987 the value of common stocks was reduced by approximately 30%. . . . Instead, the Report attempts to reconstruct the trading activity . . . and analyze how the trading systems . . . may have contributed to the rapidity and depth of the market decline."[6] The report suggested that "the character of the [stock] market has changed to the point where the 'price discovery' feature of the [futures] market is leading, rather than following, price trends in the underlying markets."[7] The culprit: "the increasing use of the futures market by institutional investors"—program trading.[8]

6

An Extraordinary Man

The SEC market break report caught the attention of another financial industry odd couple. Nathan Most and a recently hired protege, Steven M. Bloom, were tasked with new-product development at the American Stock Exchange when the SEC released its report. The path that led Most, the senior of the two, to his work at the Amex had been atypical. He had graduated from UCLA with a degree in physics just prior to the Great Depression, had been in the import/export business, and had lived and travelled extensively in the Pacific. Bloom had just received a doctorate in economics from Harvard prior to joining the new-products team.

This team reflected the changes undergoing at the Amex. For most of its existence, those with degrees had rarely settled on working at the exchange. What mattered was how well you could trade stocks, and that often came by way of an intuitive feel for the market. Courting potential companies was important, but the companies wanted to know that their stock would be actively traded. Now securities were being asked to trade nontraditional assets, and the security's construction, not the issuing company, was often paramount.

Most and Bloom were fascinated by the market break report, and the two studied its more than eight hundred pages in detail, finding in it a rich vein of data, charts, diagrams, and analysis.[1] The recommendations included the need for a unified market; clearinghouses instead of separate ones for the equity, options, and futures markets; and better flow of information between markets. Most importantly to people like Most and Bloom, the report offered a rare look into regulators' mind-sets as to what new products they might be willing to approve. The SEC postulated that if specialists had a way to trade a portfolio basket in a single trade, the market might not have dropped so precipitously.[2] The SEC suggested that a new product along those lines might be welcome and meet expedited approval. Bloom excitedly told Most, "Here's an opening we can drive a truck through."[3]

Most's long and varied career had prepared him to take advantage of the opportunity. Like the Amex he worked with, Most was a survivor. His father had fled the Baltic region during a pogrom in the early twentieth century. Most had excelled in his academic work at UCLA and had begun working on a doctoral degree when the Depression forced him to leave school.

Most found employment with Getz Bros., a family-run import/export firm with extensive operations throughout the Pacific and into Asia. He sold acoustical materials used in movie theaters throughout the Pacific. Before his wedding, he worked in Shanghai, which had fallen under Japanese occupation. When he left, his boat was one of the last to leave before the Japanese closed the port. Getz's Shanghai office manager, who had remained, later died in a Japanese concentration camp.[4] After Pearl Harbor, Most left Getz and worked on applying acoustic science to submarine warfare. His job involved testing new products by venturing out into submarine-infested waters.

When the war ended, Most returned to Getz and excelled, moving into a managerial position overseeing the operations in the Philippines and Hong Kong. Most's responsibilities extended far beyond managing the inventory in the warehouses. He travelled extensively throughout the Pacific during this time, visiting Getz's factories. In this role, Most learned two things that would be essential to his later financial operations. He learned to inspect an entire process, from raw materials to completed product, to ensure its quality, and he learned to transfer ownership of a commodity without having to deliver it.[5] Through his work in international shipping, Most also began to develop good relationships with merchant bankers, who taught him more about the financial side of his business.

Unfortunately, Most had a falling-out with the Lazarus family, which ran Getz in the late fifties, that culminated in the termination of his work with their company and the dissolution of his marriage to May Rose Lazarus. Subsequently, he experienced several other career disappointments. He emerged as an executive vice president of Pacific Vegetable Oil from 1965 to 1970, but this firm liquidated. Most then served as the executive vice president of the American Import Company from 1970 to 1974, and this led him to become president of the Pacific Commodities Exchange (PCE) from 1974 to 1976.[6] But then the PCE closed its doors. The exchange's primary product had been coconut oil futures, and a worldwide drought in the midseventies had enabled many of the traders to become millionaires—only to see their fortunes wiped out the following year when the rains returned.[7]

Most took a step backward in terms of prestige and responsibility by accepting a position as a technical assistant with the newly formed Commodity Futures Trading Commission (CFTC), created by Congress to police a market that was booming and plagued by fraudsters.[8] Most pulled up stakes and moved across the country to Washington, arriving at a pivotal point in market history. The SEC had adopted new rules ending fixed rates for brokers' commissions the year before.[9] The change was primarily aimed at the Big Board, but trading fees began to plummet on other exchanges as well.

To offset the hit to revenue, the Amex added a commodities exchange and set out to find someone to head it up.

Nathan Most had the most to offer. He knew commodities from every angle and was well versed in financing. Most was recruited away from the CFTC to become director of the Amex's newly formed office of commodity options development. In May 1977, the Amex rolled out the American Commodities Exchange (ACE) as an independent corporation to trade futures, options, and spot (cash) in both bullion and financial instruments.[10] In spite of high hopes, the new exchange failed to catch on.

In 1977, the Amex was too early in the field to make any headway against other exchanges in futures products. Strapped for cash, its American Commodities Exchange was shut down and, in 1980, sold to the New York Futures Exchange.[11] Fortunately, Most had made enough of an impression to stay at the Amex as head of its new derivatives-development effort. Nate was north of sixty, and his career had taken him throughout the Pacific, from San Francisco to New York, and from import/export executive to commodity executive, technical advisor, and security developer. The survivor with the unorthodox career track was well prepared and in place to have a profound influence on the markets.

7

The Curb

On the first anniversary of Black Friday, SEC commissioner Joseph A. Grundfest told a gathering of the Financial Executives Institute, "The long run survival and vitality of our domestic securities market does not depend primarily on the introduction of circuit breakers, prohibitions on program trading, restrictions on index arbitrage, tighter short sale restrictions, or other intrusive regulatory mechanisms. Our survival depends primarily on innovation and competition, not inhibition and regulation."[1]

At the time, large institutions were prohibited from utilizing puts, which give the holder the right to sell a security at a certain price. Instead, portfolio managers hedged with futures. From our post–2008 Great Meltdown perspective, futures shared shortcomings with credit default swaps—no one really knew how much was out there and at what levels. Grundfest opined that an arbitrary law imposed upon the markets because of a security's newness deprived the markets of data that could have been used to mitigate Black

Monday. Such admissions by regulatory agencies were, and still are, rare.

Grundfest likened program trading to selling a car part by part. The optimal trade would incorporate the technology now working its way into the exchanges and would allow the sale of a basket of stocks that would provide the market with pertinent data all in a single transaction—providing transparency. Such a security had long been the holy grail of the financial markets. In the case of the S&P 500, that would be a single, efficient, reliable trade of five hundred different stocks.

Grundfest's remarks were electrifying for people like Most and Bloom. If the Amex could create such a security and get to the finish line before the other exchanges, the potential would be enormous. Exchanges in particular were excellent security incubators because they had the largest networks of market participants. Exchange executives were in constant contact with the people on their trading floors. Joseph S. Rizzello, senior vice president of the Philadelphia Exchange, described his role as a "problem solver."[2] Investors had trades and strategies they wanted to accomplish, and the exchanges set themselves to making it happen.

New products were becoming the lifeblood for exchanges as each of them, save the New York Stock Exchange and the Nasdaq, struggled to maintain listing. A trade involving a portfolio basket might be big enough to enable an exchange to remain independent. The number of exchanges had been dwindling for some time. Philadelphia had merged with the Baltimore Exchange in 1949, the Washington Exchange in 1953, and the Pittsburgh Exchange in 1969.[3] The Chicago, Cleveland, St. Louis, and Minneapolis exchanges merged to form the Midwest Stock Exchange in 1949. (In 1993, they would resurrect the Chicago Stock Exchange name.) San Francisco and Los Angeles merged to form the Pacific Stock Exchange in 1957. These merges were caused by the joining of companies that listed on regional exchanges. Merged companies became more attractive to the Big Board, leaving local exchanges with fewer companies trading on them. Business development became imperative.

The Amex had remained independent, but that was becoming more difficult. But its street-smart mentality had served it well as it operated under the shadow of the New York Stock Exchange.

When a cartel of twenty-four brokers formed the New York Stock Exchange in 1792, they had agreed to only conduct business with each other.[4] Their exclusive club forced others to do business elsewhere. The Amex gradually emerged when these ostracized traders began meeting regularly in coffeehouses and on the street. Eventually, this mob of brokers settled upon the intersection of Wall Street and Hanover as a place where they would conduct their trades in the open air, rain or shine, throughout the entire year, even on Saturdays, enduring the oppressive heat of summer and the stinging cold of winter.

This hardy bunch became known as curbstone brokers. In a 1910 article, the *New York Times* described the common conception of the rowdy, undisciplined market: "a trading place for 'cat and dogs.'"[5] New, untested, and sometimes bogus companies introduced their securities to the public at "the Curb." Those that survived grew, matured, and often graduated to the elite indoor Big Board at the end of the block. NYSE brokers would send trades in stocks that were not listed there to the Curb for execution, providing as much as 85 percent of the Curb's business.[6] Big Board firms would often send young traders to the Curb to learn the business.

Incredible as it seems to us today, the exchange had no written rules until 1908.[7] Stocks (and their specialists) took up residence at a particular streetlamp, and traders were free to come and go. In 1920, journalist Edwin C. Hill wrote a thumbnail profile of the Curb for *Munsey's*, a quarterly magazine, in which he described the scene as a "roaring, swirling whirlpool" that should be on every tourist's list of must-see New York sites. The Curb, he wrote, "tears control of a gold-mine from an unlucky operator, and pauses to auction a puppy-dog. It is like nothing else under the astonished sky that is its only roof."[8] Between the 1920s and the 1970s, the Curb survived multiple scandals and near bankruptcy, changed its name to the American Stock Exchange, rode the ebullient wave of the "go-go years" of the 1960s, and then muddled through the dismal, go-nowhere 1970s. But hard times had now set in. Obtaining new listings was becoming more difficult, as the Nasdaq (the OTC market in the electronic age) had become a formidable competitor while Amex-listed stocks continued to migrate to the NYSE. The Amex was slowing, being crowded toward extinction.

As it became more dependent on new trading products for revenue, the Amex turned to its board of directors for ideas and advice, recruiting members who had both. One of the recruits was economist Burton G. Malkiel, author of *A Random Walk Down Wall Street*, widely regarded as one of the all-time must-read books on the efficiency of markets. Malkiel had also written several other books on options, which numerous brokers had expressed an interest in being able to trade.[9] Options were more appealing than futures, which entailed burdens such as the delivery and storage of commodities and buying and selling from institutional traders. The options market was primarily retail, which typically meant higher margins, and was settled in cash instead of in the delivery of the underlying asset. The Amex board sought and received permission from the SEC and the newly formed Commodity Futures Trading Commission (CFTC).

Malkiel, whose professional colleagues included mutual fund pioneer Jack Bogle of Vanguard and index fund pioneer Mac McQuown of Wells Fargo, chaired the Amex's New Product Development Committee, created in 1981 to explore how to take advantage of the coming expiration of the SEC's moratorium on options.[10] The SEC was treating options the same way it did stocks—the exchange that was awarded the right to trade options for a company stock had it exclusively.

Malkiel suggested the Amex consider options in four areas:

1. Precious metals
2. Treasury securities
3. Nongovernment debt securities
4. Stocks that did not already have options trading on them[11]

During the next five years, the Amex grew the trading volume of its stock options to surpass the NYSE and the CBOE; issued options on Treasury-related products; and introduced the Major Market Index (MMI), comprised of twenty blue-chip stocks, to serve as a proxy for the Dow Jones Industrials. Index-based investing became well established, and by 1986, the Amex had nearly quadrupled its trade volume.

The final piece in the product development team was Ivers W. Riley, hired from the New York Stock Exchange in 1987 and appointed senior executive vice president of all derivatives activity, making him Nathan Most's boss.[12] Riley had also worked at the CBOE, where he had been a vocal advocate and the driving force to have puts listed on exchanges, earning him the moniker "Mr. Puts."[13] Like Nathan Most, Riley was an alum of UCLA, where he had studied finance. With Malkiel, Riley, Most, and Bloom, the Amex had the equivalent of a Yankees first team in the development of index investing and ETFs.

8

A Spider Is Born

Ivers Riley proved to be the right person to lead the development that resulted in the ETF. Joseph B. Stefanelli, an executive VP at the exchange, recalled that Riley was quick to grasp new ideas and supportive of those who had them. Stefanelli said that when Most and Bloom first brought the ETF concept to Riley, "he just told Nate, 'Start working on it and whatever you need, you let me know and we'll get this done.'"[1]

Nathan Most was seventy-three years old when he got the idea that became today's biggest traded security.[2] The date the idea popped into his head is uncertain, but it may well have been in the months following Black Monday. It was inspired by his experience with those commodity depository receipts: paper backed by warehouses full of coconuts or tin or greasy wool—or any of a hundred other common and obscure commodities.[3] Most's contribution could have included the name of this new product: Standard & Poor's depository receipt, or SPDR.

A new security required seed money, and Vanguard seemed like a natural fit to the Amex team. Most took the train to Pennsylvania to meet with Vanguard's Bogle, a meeting set up by Malkiel.[4] In just fifteen years, Vanguard had become a major force in retail investments committed to indexing. Surely Vanguard would understand the value of a security such as the Spider.

But it was clear, in Bogle's eyes, that the idea for the security was designed principally to generate volume for the Amex.[5] He noted several flaws and told Most that Vanguard would pass. Bogle recalled later that he was concerned the Spiders would encourage individual investors to stray from the buy-and-hold strategy he favored and engage in excessive trading that would be costly and have tax consequences.

But Most and Bloom were not ready to give up on their idea. They had something big, if they could just iron out the kinks—and they weren't the only ones stalking the holy grail.

9

The Philadelphia Foray

Among Most and Bloom's competitors were luminaries at the Philadelphia Exchange, members of a venerable and respected national institution. For much of Philadelphia's history, it had led the way. As the nation's first seat of government, the city boasts a long list of firsts—the first library, hospital, medical school, insurance firm, commercial bank, initial public offering, and paved road—and was the home of the First Bank of the United States and the US Mint. Likewise, the Philadelphia Board of Brokers was the oldest stock exchange in America, established in 1790, two years before the New York Stock Exchange.[1]

The Philadelphia Exchange was prominent well into the nineteenth century, serving as the venue for raising much of the capital that financed the nation's railroads, but with the opening of the Erie Canal, the New York Stock Exchange emerged as the nation's new financial center. The bankruptcy of the Penn Central in 1970 appeared to be the final nail in the in the exchange's coffin.[2] Many also assumed that a merger with the NYSE was inevitable.

The consolidation of several other regional exchanges into the Philadelphia Exchange couldn't stem the decline; only eighty-eight firms were listed when all was said and done. If companies merged with Philadelphia-based firms, the surviving company would often opt for listing on the New York Stock Exchange. Yet despite these struggles and headwinds, the Philadelphia Exchange experienced an unexpected resurgence in the 1970s.

The future looked as bleak as possible in 1971 when the board recruited Nicholas A. Giordano to become CFO.[3] Giordano had worked for accounting firm Price Waterhouse after college and for several years at a brokerage; then he caught the eye of Philadelphia Exchange president Elkins Wetherill. Giordano was two years shy of his thirtieth birthday. Giordano joined the Philadelphia Exchange and, for a time, helped Wetherill revitalize the exchange by bringing in new revenue through the options market.

In 1973, a group of futures traders comprising the Chicago Board of Trade chartered the Chicago Board Options Exchange (CBOE), an exchange dedicated to option trading.[4] For the Philadelphia Exchange, options offered a seemingly endless number of new securities. A company such as GE would not have a single option but many. The seemingly limitless combinations of varying strike prices ($50, $51, $52) and expiration dates (June 30, September 30), all of which would expire, ensured continuous trading volume, especially for the most widely traded stocks. A further attractive feature (which no longer exists) was that, for a period of time, exchanges were awarded exclusive rights to a company's options.

Sensing the potential, Wetherill sent his product development team to meet with the CBOE in 1973. By early 1975, the Philadelphia Exchange believed they had the necessary pieces in place and had filed a request with the SEC for approval to buy and sell options. The American Stock Exchange followed suit soon after. For undisclosed reasons, the SEC approved the Amex's request first, allowing it to get a jump on recruiting issuers. The Philadelphia Exchange (PHLX) now faced an uphill fight for market share. But in June 1975, the PHLX began trading options on a dedicated floor.[5] Options trading on the Philadelphia Exchange grew from $570 million in 1978 to more than $5 billion in 1983, and its market share in this new field grew from 3 to 9 percent.[6] For the Amex, the options-trading boom made it necessary to relocate for space and to gain access to state-of-the-art infrastructure.

10

Turf Wars

In 1982, Giordano's team at the PHLX offered a new option tied to the exchange rate between currencies—a security so groundbreaking that they required the approval not only of the SEC but of Congress as well.[1] These options were an immediate hit with investors and companies involved in import/export trade as a way to hedge their currency risk. Prior to the new currency options, companies had had to execute contracts with their counterparties. These contracts may have looked good on paper but often were expensive and difficult to unwind if needed. A currency option was standardized and merely required the holder to purchase an offsetting position to the one he or she held. A buyer of a call could sell an offsetting call. A seller of a call could buy an offsetting one. Things looked promising until the CFTC objected to trading these securities on an options exchange rather than a futures one.

The SEC had given its blessing to currency options. But the CFTC, joined by the Chicago Mercantile Exchange (CME), challenged the SEC's jurisdiction.[2] The CFTC argued that what PHLX called an option was really a futures contract, something over which the CFTC exercised exclusive jurisdiction. The CME claimed that it was already trading similar products and that the PHLX currency options were a threat to its revenue. The PHLX and their innovation had become mired in the turf war between the SEC and the newly formed CFTC.

The roots of CTFC's objection lay in the history of the Chicago Board of Trade (CBOT), where principal farm commodities had been traded since 1848.[3] Initially, the CBOT was a "spot" market, meaning products were sold for cash. Later, in 1851, the first futures contract in the US traded in Chicago for three thousand bushels of corn.[4] It was logical that the market should be regulated by the Agriculture Department and that Chicago, the hub of the nation's breadbasket, should be the center of futures trading. The SEC oversaw securities trading in New York, and futures trading was centered in Chicago and—beginning in 1974—overseen by CFTC.

The SEC and CFTC had each developed their own rules and regulations, and neither was interested in ceding authority over what each believed to be their rightful jurisdiction.

The PHLX was encroaching upon an area that the CFTC believed was theirs to regulate. Meanwhile, the CBOT had developed a new futures contract tied to the Government National Mortgage Association (Ginnie Mae) bond as the underlying security.[5] Trading in the underlying bond was clearly under the scope of the SEC, but the CFTC claimed jurisdiction over the contract—a futures contract. Eager to assert themselves in these new futures, the CBOT dispatched its attorney to Washington to jawbone congressional members and staff, claiming the CFTC should have exclusive jurisdiction over all futures trading, regardless of the underlying asset.

Fortunately for the CFTC, Congress was already in the process of hammering out the commission's scope and substance. Perhaps unwittingly, the CFTC was granted exclusive authority over all futures and required any forward contract to trade on an exchange over which the CFTC had jurisdiction.[6,7] It held that authority for the next decade, until the appearance of currency options, which were neither securities (to be traded on stock exchanges) nor commodities (to be traded on futures exchanges). Eventually, the attorneys and leaders of the CFTC and the SEC, as well as the exchanges, were able to hammer out their differences and bring clarity to the issue. The CME and the Philadelphia Exchange were permitted to keep their respective options.

The next turf war between the regulators developed over futures on indexes and individual stocks. Once again, both the SEC and CFTC claimed exclusive jurisdiction. The two sides were at an impasse until it was resolved by a rare case of regulatory mediation between the two heads of the respective commissions—Phil Johnson, chair of the CFTC, and John Shad, chair of the SEC—in December of 1981.[8] The agreement they reached that December came to be known as the Shad-Johnson Accord, later codified as part of the Commodity Exchange Act.[9] Futures on broad-based indexes would trade on CFTC-regulated exchanges, whereas futures on most individual stocks and bonds were to be banned, with some exceptions for such instruments as government bonds.[10]

But the pace of innovation in the financial markets was occurring at breakneck speed, and it was clearly outpacing the ability of Congress or regulators to oversee it in an organized and logical fashion. With so much uncertainty regarding regulatory scope, innovative exchanges ran the risk of venturing away from the safe harbor their respective regulators provided, and Giordano at the PHLX was already working on new products.

The CBOE introduced the first option on a stock index in 1983.[11] Investors could now invest in, or hedge against, a basket of stocks with only a minimal amount. Vanguard had only introduced the first index mutual fund in 1975, and now, just eight years later, investors could buy an option on the same underlying index. Giordano had found his next idea.

11

Problem Solvers and Trailblazers

The OEX option on the S&P 500 would prove to be one of the most successful options of all time.[1] Giordano saw an opening to develop an underlying security for the OEX option. Novice traders especially would be attracted to a security that could be matched with or hedged against the corresponding option. Giordano grasped that the proposed security's potential was enormous. He challenged his staff—which by 1985 included Joseph S. Rizzello, head of product development, and William W. Uchimoto, the exchange's compliance attorney—to create it.[2] Giordano intended it to look like a stock in all aspects: pay a dividend, trade throughout the day, track its net asset value closely, and be capable of being shorted. If successful, the Philadelphia Exchange would have the first exchange-traded fund.

In the late 1960s, Rizzello, head of the PHLX product development effort, had worked at Drexel Harriman Ripley, a firm that specialized in underwriting equity and fixed-income securities.[3] With his intimate knowledge of the operations and systems underlying the trading, he was familiar with what a security had to do functionally so that it could trade on the exchange.[4]

Competition between the exchanges was brutal. Being first to market might ensure that you would be the sole trader of a security, or it might at least enable you to develop a critical lead in trade volume (and thus profits). Liquidity had a habit of attracting further liquidity, as traders were confident they could open or close their positions when they wanted or needed to. Also, greater liquidity translated into lower costs. In the exchanges, whether a market was trending upward, downward, or even flat, an exchange that enjoyed healthy trade volume made money. The new trading model required new securities, unlike the old model, which called for new company listings.

Giordano's new currency option was a feather in his cap, but the portfolio basket that would trade like a stock was always in the back of his mind. While it is a common misconception that exchange product development teams directed their focus to one or two items at a time, this was the usual approach. They might already have several irons in the fire when an even more promising idea arose, often coming from a trader who had a trade or strategy they could not execute. Exchange product development teams were problem solvers, and exchanges always had some type of problem.

The PHLX team made several critical decisions in the development of Giordano's portfolio basket idea. First, the

PHLX team chose to base their basket on an existing index instead of creating one themselves. They decided upon the S&P 500, which was becoming well known among investors because McGraw Hill, owner of the index, had licensed the index to Vanguard for their mutual funds.[5] Next, they decided to go with a computer-driven model to optimize the index instead of holding all of its stocks. Today, we would give this decision little thought, but back in the mideighties, the necessary technology and equipment were relatively new, expensive, and of unproven reliability.

Optimizing the S&P 500 would make the operation of the basket cheaper and more manageable because it would involve fewer stocks. More importantly, by making the differences between the optimized portfolio and the S&P 500 significant enough, the PHLX could avoid paying licensing fees to McGraw Hill. But a chance encounter at a road show for their new product, which they were naming cash index participation (CIP) shares, made it clear they would be courting a legal challenge. An attorney for McGraw Hill, owner of Standard & Poor's, warned them, "This is our product even though you have changed four or five stocks."[6] Not wanting to be embroiled in an expensive, time-consuming legal battle (one that would allow competitors to step in), the PHLX licensed the S&P 500.

Regulators and Competitors

To bring a security to market, you had to have the SEC on board. Uchimoto, the PHLX's corporate counsel, had previously worked at the SEC in their market structure group, and he brought to the team valuable insights and beneficial connections with the regulator. In addition to his product development duties at the PHLX, Uchimoto also served as counsel to the exchange's two subsidiaries, the Stock Clearing Corporation of Philadelphia and the Philadelphia Depository Trust Corporation.[1] Giordano, Rizzello, and Uchimoto travelled together so often to promote the new securities that, in spite of Uchimoto's obvious Japanese heritage, they came to be known as "the three Italians from Philly."[2]

The PHLX wanted trading and pricing of its cash index participation shares to be as transparent as possible. This extended even to the name they chose for the shares. CIP would not be collateralized with the underlying stocks in the index, so all trades would settle in cash, not in the delivery of the stocks in the index. Like a stock, CIP would pay quarterly dividends generated from the stocks, and the security would have no expiration date.[3] But instead of clearing like a stock, trades would be cleared through the Options Clearing Corporation (OCC) in Chicago. The security was truly a hybrid and would most likely catch the attention of the SEC and the CFTC, both jealously guarding their jurisdictions.

In March 1988, just five months after Black Monday, Uchimoto filed legal documents with the SEC, seeking approval of the PHLX's new CIP product. The regulatory process was notoriously long, tedious, and expensive. The PHLX needed exemptions from provisions in two different laws, the Securities Act of 1933 and the Securities Exchange Act of 1934. To avoid revealing its strategy to competitors, the exchange first submitted preliminary paperwork for review under a confidentiality agreement.[4]

When it came time to submit the formal prospectus to the SEC, the Administrative Procedure Act (APA) required that such filings be made public. At the time, patent protections did not exist for securities, so staying under the radar as long as possible was vital. Exchanges and financial companies vigilantly followed new filings with the SEC, dissecting them, picking out what was useful, and copying it. This is what happened to Philadelphia's CIP filing.

Up in New York at the Amex, as soon as Nathan Most and Steven Bloom got their hands on the PHLX prospectus, they did what any product development team worth their salt would do when a more viable product appeared. Within just two months, the AMEX team had rolled out its own basket product, called equity index participation (EIP) certificates. Elsewhere, the CBOE developed its own version, value of index participation (VIP) certificates.

The plagiarism was both brazen and sloppy; a typo in the Philadelphia Exchange's prospectus showed up in the Amex's.[5] The Philadelphia team had spent two-plus years developing their version, but the Amex team had copied it and gone to market in just two months.

Of course, regulators erupted into their own competition over PHLX's idea. The CFTC claimed that CIP was a futures contract and was therefore under its jurisdiction. The SEC countered that the CIP was a security and thus would remain under its jurisdiction.[6] The Investment Company Institute (ICI), the trade group for the mutual fund industry, became the third dog in the fight. The new products were potentially a competitive threat to mutual funds, who held a nice pseudomonopoly on portfolio-based investing, so the institute filed with the courts. The ICI claimed that the new products properly fell under the Investment Company Act of 1940 and, like mutual funds, should not be allowed to trade on any exchange.

The mutual fund industry worried that the CIP would enjoy an advantage of intraday pricing over mutual funds.[7]

They also worried that investors would see the benefit of being able to buy a portfolio of stocks without having to pay for those stocks to be, in effect, "warehoused" in mutual fund portfolios. That option would likely drive down mutual fund pricing and profits

The horses were lined up in the gates, and the race was on. The Amex took the early lead by many lengths. On the first day, the Amex traded more than 40,000 of their EIP contracts versus 545 contracts on the Philadelphia Exchange for their CIP shares.[8]

Stung, the PHLX filed a cease and desist letter against the Amex, claiming a copyright violation.[9] The Amex acknowledged that it had used CIP as its model but had made a material modification: whereas the CIP only allowed for cash delivery, the Amex and its EIP allowed for physical delivery of the stocks as well.

Before the courts could rule on that issue, an appellate panel in Chicago settled the jurisdictional dispute, finding that the PHLX product had enough of an options component that it fell within the purview of Commodity Futures Trading Commission, not the Securities Exchange Commission.[10] Giordano later lamented that the ruling was "a major step backward in the regulation and development of innovative new products."[11]

It was frustrating to career investment professionals that federal judges, who were not financial professionals and were unschooled in the intricacies of innovative products, were adjudicating the boundaries between the SEC and CFTC. The PHLX team felt abandoned by the SEC, which did not defend their product as strongly as the PHLX had hoped.

The short life and swift demise of the CIP cast a pall over the Philadelphia Exchange. The new-products team continued to design and introduce new securities with catchy acronyms—DIBS, OWLS, RISKS, and DORS—but none held the promethean promise of the CIP. In the years that followed, Giordano, Rizzello, and Uchimoto moved on to other endeavors, and the Philadelphia Exchange gradually faded until 2007, when the remaining business was absorbed by Nasdaq, the once upstart. Today, the last vestige of our nation's oldest exchange exists at the tail end of an acronym: NASDAQ OMX PHLX.[12]

13

Forensic Aftermath

Meanwhile, other innovators were still reeling from Black Monday and trying to adjust. In the weeks immediately after the 1987 crash, Berkeley professor Hayne Leland told a *Fortune* writer that he had long been "intrigued by the role of uncertainty in markets."[1] He and his business partners, John O'Brien and Mark Rubinstein, had just been clobbered by the Wall Street media—and not a few port-folio managers—for their role in contributing to a historic episode of uncertainty in the markets.

Leland, O'Brien, and Rubinstein had, for several years, been developing and preaching the gospel of what was then a novel tactic for portfolio hedging: portfolio insurance. Although the crash had multiple causes, much of the blame had settled on them. No one would have been surprised had their firm, LOR, been hounded out of business. But some of their clients got the protection they paid for, and half the $60 billion that LOR had covered before the crash stuck with them after.[2] Leland and his partners stood undaunted, more intrigued by uncertainty in the markets than anything else. When asked when the team had begun refining their strategy, Leland responded, "The following morning."[3]

One element of their solution was inspired by an experimental product introduced in 1983 by Americus Shareowner Services Corporation.[4] Its Americus Trust was the vehicle, and in retrospect, the tactic presaged the collateralized debt obligations that played a central role in the Great Meltdown of 2008. Investors exchanged shares of AT&T stock for a unit in the Americus Trust. Each unit had two severable parts—prime and score—each of which were listed and could trade on the American Stock Exchange.[5, 6] Unit holders could sell one and keep the other to fit their investment strategy.

The prime part of the unit entitled holders to dividends paid by AT&T stock held in the trust plus appreciation of the shares up to a predetermined price—generally about 20 to 25 percent above the stock's price when the units were created. It was a hybrid security, guaranteeing income with a stock option attached. The score part of the units entitled holders to capital appreciation above the predetermined value by a predetermined termination date—a stock option.

The Americus Trust idea was intended to address the impending breakup of AT&T, the company that had had a monopoly on North American phone service for seven decades and the most widely held stock in the world. After a decade of legal wrangling with the federal government, the company was in the process of the court-ordered divestiture, which would eventually convert a reliable, dividend-paying blue chip into seven smaller regional companies with uncertain financials and futures.[7] AT&T had long been a bedrock in the portfolios of the most conservative investors and managers—a "widows and orphans" favorite. Determining the postbreakup value was a daunting process, and the first Americus Trust was designed to appeal both to conservative managers and to more aggressive investors who were speculating that the pieces of AT&T would prove to be worth more than the whole.

The options aspect of the units had a five-year expiration date. Unfortunately for the Americus Trusts (others were created for stocks like Texaco), in 1986 the IRS ruled that the trust was a taxable entity separate from its investors, thus exposing unit holders to double taxation and erasing the appeal. Only twenty-seven Americus Trusts were created.[8]

But Leland, O'Brien, and Rubinstein had a second source of inspiration: a fellow Berkeley professor, Nils H. Hakansson. Hakansson had published a paper in the *Financial Analysts Journal* on a concept he called a "purchasing power fund."[9] He proposed that such a fund would hold an investment such as the S&P 500 Index with the entire spectrum of possible returns over a set time period mapped out and divided into various segments. Then shares in the trust representing each of these segments would be sold to investors, who could select specific segments of the return spectrum. Hakansson termed these SuperShares.

LOR decided to provide two funds: one with the S&P 500 Index as the underlying asset, the other with a money market. Each of these funds, known as SuperUnits, would be divided into two outcomes, as had been done with the Americus Trusts. For the S&P 500 Index, the returns would be for a bull market and a moderate market. The money market fund would also be separated into a flat market and a bear market. LOR's four SuperShares had return characteristics of four basic investment strategies: call option (appreciation SS); covered call write (priority SS); bond (income and residual SS); and a collateralized put (protection SS). The overall strategy was called the SuperTrust. It was, as one expert put it, "a deconstructed S&P 500 option that included a money market fund, an S&P 500 option, a volatility unit, and an S&P 500 Trust."[10]

The SuperTrust required no margin or counterparty. SuperShare holders were not at the market's mercy to have their strategy executed like LOR had been when they had pursued their portfolio insurance strategy with futures. Instead, holders could match their risk profile with the appropriate outcome. Unlike puts and calls, SuperShares did not need to be rolled over quarterly, thus keeping expenses lower. Though some shares had characteristics of options, each was designed to trade on a stock exchange—instead of the much smaller (and hence much less robust) futures and options exchanges.

The final element involved in the SuperTrust solved the issue of allowing these various securities to trade on an exchange and yet not deviate from their net asset value as a closed-end fund would. LOR's attorneys identified a solution that was simple yet brilliant. If a mutual fund vehicle were required to maintain a trading price close to or at the net asset value, offer a mutual fund. Next, if this mutual fund could not trade on an exchange, issue a security that could. LOR chose a security that was a unit investment trust (UIT), an investment vehicle defined in the Securities Act of 1933, the law governing securities in the US. UITs could trade on an exchange, but they could not manage or alter their portfolio over time. By only buying shares of the mutual fund, the UIT was compliant with the Securities Act as having a fixed portfolio. The mutual fund would only invest in the S&P 500 and was a pass-through to the UIT.

As simple as this solution seemed, it was difficult for the SEC to get its arms around this construction. Adding an element of the SuperTrust with its severable SuperUnits greatly complicated things for the regulators, and this resulted in steep legal fees as LOR sought to educate them. When they had to review Hakasson's spectrum of returns as well, many investors—as well as some investment professionals—were bewildered.

Amazingly, Leland, O'Brien, and Rubinstein had focused their thoughts, developed their ideas, and crafted the SuperTrust in just over a year since Black Monday. To obtain SEC approval for the SuperTrust and SuperShares, LOR sought what is known as a "no-action letter"—an approval of a proposed investment security based upon the precedent of a similar security—from the SEC Division of Investment Management in December of 1988. LOR based their request on the Americus Trust as the precedent, but they were rejected in early 1989.[11] So LOR was forced to file an exemption request. Before finally obtaining approval in July 1990, LOR submitted five amendments in addition to its initial request for exemption. LOR received their exemption $4 million in legal fees later, paving the way for them to register a new security called the Index Trust SuperUnit, another game-changing and individual-friendly innovation in ways to invest in the market.[12]

14

The Canadian Collaboration

Innovators in the United States weren't the only ones working on a new way to trade a basket of stocks. Two months after the federal court halted CIP, the Toronto Futures Exchange (TFE)—the futures trading floor of the Toronto Stock Exchange—announced its own new product, the Toronto 35 index participation shares (TIPs).[1] It differed significantly from the similarly named cash index participation (CIP) units, but the "index participation" resonated with investors and traders and was thus incorporated into the name. While competition inside a single country could be fierce, exchanges in different countries enjoyed a free flow of ideas, as they did not consider themselves to be competitors.

The mirror opposite of Philadelphia's declining exchange, Toronto was eclipsing the Montreal Exchange to become Canada's premier exchange. But like its American counterparts, Toronto was looking to increase trading on the floor, a need made more pressing by Canada being about one-ninth the size of the United States in population.

Heading up the Canadian effort was Andrew Clademenos, whose primary qualification was his law degree from the University of Toronto Faculty of Law. Toronto's futures exchange was relatively new, and Clademenos was charged with drafting its bylaws. Later, he became head of product development, where one of his roles was to "corral members and win them over to the new products."[2]

The United States already had fifteen years of index-based investing, but the concept was virtually nonexistent in Canada. The concentration of Canada's economy around several sectors (primarily banking and commodities) meant that, historically, investors had not been interested in the full market, merely in those sectors—and not everything in those sectors, only the winners.

Sensing this view was changing, the Toronto Exchange created two indexes, the TSE 300 and the TSE 100. However, these were merely benchmarks. They proved to be too large, with far too many illiquid stocks to be the underlying portfolios for successful derivative products.[3] The team created a smaller optimized portfolio of thirty-five stocks—the TSE 35—that reflected their overall market. This proved to be far more liquid and thus more attractive to the traders on the floor.

With a vastly improved index, Clademenos believed potential trading opportunities existed beyond the usual assortment of futures and options. One Friday afternoon, he was brainstorming with several members when Andy Morgan, a trader from the investment bank Gordon Capital, suggested that they create a product for the TSE 35 similar to an American depositary receipt (ADR). Andy was quite familiar with these securities, having employed them while trading in London prior to coming over to Canada. With clients with investments in places such as South Africa, Australia, Hong Kong, Canada, and London, ADRs had proved to be a highly efficient way for Andy and others to trade stocks that might have conflicting settlement dates at their respective exchanges and might require weeks afterward to deliver the certificates.

The appeal of such a product for the new index was unmistakable, and Clademenos assembled a team of exchange members to develop one and bring it to market. The team included not only competitors in the exchange but also members from different regulators. This interdisciplinary collaboration, which enabled the product to be designed and launched with remarkable speed, came to be considered the hallmark of TIPs.

The development team worked together to address issues such as how trades would make their way to the exchange floor, how they were to be executed quickly and efficiently, and the upgraded record keeping that would be required to trade thirty-five stocks simultaneously. Perhaps learning from Philadelphia's recent misfortune,

TIPs would be fully collateralized. The team developed a creation/redemption mechanism that would allow the TIPs to trade close to net asset value (NAV). "This," according to Andrew Clademenos, "was the true breakthrough that made the TIPs possible."[4] To accomplish this on the trading floor, though, required the market maker to physically walk around the floor to accumulate the necessary stocks to create the units.[5] The computer systems then available were not capable of handling that aspect.

Black Monday had kicked off some of the greatest years of innovation the financial markets ever witnessed, but this innovation was not without its obstacles. The Philadelphia Exchange filed its CIP application and wound up in court; Leland, O'Brien, and Rubinstein (LOR) filed their initial SuperTrust no-action letter with the SEC only to enter into a protracted regulatory quagmire; and the Toronto Exchange had to file their TIPs application with the Ontario Security Commission (OSC). Ontario faced fewer complications than its fellows in the US. LOR and the PHLX had each become embroiled in a legal or regulatory morass, but not so Ontario. The Canadian exchange encountered no delays or skepticism from the regulators and no serious resistance from the mutual fund and derivatives industries.

The consequences for the US markets were far reaching. While the SEC impeded both LOR and the Amex with numerous delays in the form of "requests for more information," the OSC provided feedback and guidance to the Toronto team. The northern exchange received their approval from the OSC in November 1989, a mere two months after submitting their initial application. Detractors accused the Canadian regulators of approving a security they did not truly understand, but the TIPs launched without a hitch, so perhaps the contempt is undeserved.

The Canadian mutual fund industry was unable to mount any successful opposition to the TIPs. They might not have been pleased that Toronto's proposed security would be allowed to lend shares for short selling, something prohibited to mutual funds; this concession from the OSC provided an additional source of revenue for TIPs and was a major reason why the fund's MER (the Canadian expense ratio) was below zero for a while. But the OSC did not consider security lending a competitive advantage they were granting to TIPs over mutual funds; they considered it an innovation that benefitted ordinary investors. The promise of TIPs was never realized; the fund was never able to gain traction with Canadian retail investors. But the cannon had been fired: the Canadians were poised to launch the first ETF.

15

The Race to Market

The Ontario Exchange launched the TIPs on March 9, 1990.[1] The launch occurred without a single hitch and was a success. Toronto led the way in executing the first trade of a portfolio of stocks on an exchange floor in a security that would not significantly deviate from its net asset value throughout the day. In keeping with their retail focus, the shares were valued at one-tenth of the index.[2] Despite these efforts, not one dollar of the first $150 million that flowed into TIPs was retail. "After the first few days, it [the TIPs] wasn't going gangbusters," said Clademenos. "But the TIPs was never at risk of being closed."[3]

The first ETF to trade on an exchange had several differences from its modern counterparts. As mentioned before, the market maker would walk around the Toronto Exchange to accumulate the stocks needed to create TIPs shares. Creations and redemptions occurred only once a quarter, as TIPs resembled European options, which may only be exercised at the end of the quarter. Initially, this posed no problem, as the vast majority of the money going into the fund was institutional, and settlement periods were longer than they are today.

Surprisingly, however, the Canadian success brought no new entrants into the ETF arena, at least not for several years. PHLX was no longer pursuing any similar products, leaving only LOR and the American Stock Exchange to continue their work.

Nathan Most and Steven Bloom had continued to make progress on their Spider, and the Amex filed the Spider with the SEC in June of 1990.[4] As head of product development, Most often met with financial firms, seeking new products to trade on the exchange or pitching products already trading. Among others, he met with Leland, O'Brien, and Rubinstein about their SuperTrust and with Robert Tull, the Morgan Stanley executive who had headed up the firm's new order-execution system just in time for Black Monday, about the new products he was now developing.

Tull and Most met for lunch in early 1990, soon after the TIPs had launched.[5] Most wanted to know if Tull thought a product like TIPs was possible in the US. The question was coy. The Amex filed the Spider with the SEC several months after the lunch. That filing injected some urgency into Tull's work on a similar product for Morgan Stanley.

Morgan Stanley Trust, for which Tull had designed the trading platform, was one of the two new strategic business lines that Morgan Stanley was building in the late 1980s and early 1990s. The firm had clients with high net worths in countries throughout Europe and the Americas, but international trusts were complex. A multinational trust division would have thousands of securities, many of which traded on multiple exchanges at differing prices and currencies. Tax rates differed between countries, and countries treated citizens and foreigners differently. Morgan Stanley Trust managed assets across a myriad of political and tax boundaries, with beneficiaries, fiduciaries, and tax collectors all relying on the trust accounting system, which had to be the ultimate in record keeping.

Morgan Stanley's second new line of business was program trading, which involved the simultaneous execution of a large number of stock trades that were typically triggered by an index's price movement. Program trading often employed derivatives to generate excess returns, which explains why, even though it involved the selling of stocks, it operated under the derivatives trading unit. It had been used extensively on Black Monday and, as has been noted, was considered by some to be one of the primary causes of the market's precipitous decline that day. As program trading sought to exploit price discrepancies between indexes and their underlying stocks by executing trades on separate exchanges, Morgan Stanley found it to be a very profitable business.

In 1986, Morgan Stanley had signed a licensing agreement with Capital International for use of the international indexes for several countries throughout Europe and Asia. By the late 1980s, Morgan Stanley Capital International (MSCI) had the rights to the dominant country index for every nation in which investors had an appetite, save for the UK, where FTSE was dominant.[6] MSCI was the most recognized product line for investing in individual countries. Likewise, it held the dominant international index, the Europe, Australia, and Far East (EAFE) Index.

Now, with all the innovation in the financial markets, Morgan Stanley planned a new security to combine their two new business lines, program trading and international indexes. The firm wanted a product that would meet five key goals:

1. Deliver equity returns
2. Receive uniform tax treatment in all major markets
3. Engage various business segments at the firm to achieve company-wide buy-in
4. Leverage the firm's strengths across product lines
5. Be patentable[7]

To achieve these goals, Robert Tull set about studying the prospectuses of TIPs, SuperTrust, and, later, the Spider. What he learned proved instrumental in creating the optimized portfolio as listed securities (OPALS).

While the Amex was starting from relative scratch in creating a stand-alone product—the Spider—Tull aimed for a product that would involve many units of Morgan Stanley. As OPALS would use the MSCI indexes comprised of internationals stocks, some of which would have no liquidity, the portfolios would be optimized and computers would determine the best subset of the index shares to hold based on cost, market capitalization, liquidity, industry weightings, and comparable returns.

OPALS would not be a fund like the Spider; it would be a debt instrument issued by Morgan Stanley that, instead of paying a rate of interest, would pay out the portfolio's return—its appreciation and dividends. As such, OPALS were a precursor to the exchange-traded notes we have today. Tull achieved his patent goal with the OPALs, something that eluded the Spider, SuperTrust, and TIPs. OPALS would later serve as the basis for an exchange-traded product that was to be far more consequential in the ETF's development, but that was several years later.

"Bob Tull was the brains of OPALS," said Paul Aaronson, an attorney from Morgan Stanley's London office who would later head OPALS. "He reminded me of [LOR's] John O'Brien. Both men were visionaries who could bring complex problems and issues together."[8]

Another new product had been launched, and the history of the ETF was well underway. As 1992 wound down, the financial industry was entering one of its most fruitful periods ever. Three important new securities would launch over a six-month period—one by a registered investment advisor (RIA), one by an investment bank, and one by an exchange.

16

A Brilliant Failure

As the Toronto Exchange launched TIPs and Morgan Stanley launched OPALs, Nathan Most and the Amex team served as both spectators and participants in the flurry of activity occurring in the financial markets. As the team watched how quickly TIPs went to market and Most met periodically with Tull over lunch, it was clear that time was of the essence in developing the Spider.

As team leader Ivers Riley put it, the Amex team hoped to design a security "that would look, taste, smell, and feel like a share of stock representing the whole market."[1] But the path ahead was riddled with obstacles. Both the futures industry and the mutual fund industry were invested in making sure a product like the Spider never came to market. The futures industry contended that any basket offering had to be backed up by physical securities, while the mutual fund industry remained doggedly defensive of any suspected infringement on its turf. A product like the Spider had never been seen before. While Riley, Most, and Bloom tried to obtain SEC approval for their fund, they had to toe a fine line to avoid being classed with futures or a mutual fund trading on an exchange. Although the Amex was focused on the Spider, they were also looking for new securities to trade. SuperTrust had caught their attention, not only in the way that they were working to obtain SEC approval. The Amex believed the SuperTrust had securities that might trade on the Amex floor. Initially, LOR had intended the SuperTrust to list on the NYSE, but Riley contacted O'Brien to see if they would consider listing on the Amex. According to O'Brien, Riley said the Amex was willing to promote the SuperTrust "to the tune of $1 million."[2, 3] Whatever the content of that conversation, however, in the end, the SuperTrust agreed to list on the Amex instead of the more prestigious NYSE.

Unfortunately, what had looked like a promising deal fell through when LOR's SuperTrust encountered another obstacle. The CBOE claimed that several of the securities embedded in the SuperTrust were options and should trade on an options exchange. They were prepared to contest the listing in court. Although LOR was convinced that all of the six securities in the SuperTrust should trade on a stock exchange, which was their intent and part of their strategy, they could not afford additional legal fees. LOR was a partnership, two of the members being academics, and they needed SuperTrust to generate revenue. They acquiesced to the CBOE's threat, and four of the securities listed on its option exchange. With securities trading on separate exchanges, the SuperTrust became less attractive to the Amex and to the traders.

The SuperTrust concept and products were received with a great deal of head scratching, skepticism, and disdain. Five months before the actual launch, Floyd Norris, lead financial writer of the *New York Times*, wrote, "Is Wall Street ready for the 'son of portfolio insurance'?" Norris reported that big index fund managers were proving hard to entice: "The offering must overcome a stunning complexity that has caused some to shy away. 'You're going to explain that? Good luck,' said a senior official at one brokerage firm that decided against being an underwriter."[4]

LOR's SuperTrust finally launched on November 5, 1992. Initial subscriptions reached almost $2 billion (in constant dollars)—half of the goal, but nevertheless a record at the time and an amazing accomplishment given the complexity of the SuperTrust and the hurdles LOR had encountered. But trading of the securities never caught on. They languished on the floors of the Amex and the CBOE for over two years until LOR threw in the towel, liquidating the fund when it matured in 1995.

Still, SuperTrust's failure had been a brilliant one. The securities had blazed a trail—in design and in their handling of the SEC—and the Amex especially had benefitted from their work. When the Spider launched successfully just over two months after SuperTrust, it proved the veracity of the old adage "the early bird gets the worm, but the second mouse gets the cheese."

— 17 —

The Hail Mary Security

The Amex's Spider had many similarities with LOR's SuperTrust, especially in regard to delivering stock market returns to investors with an exchange-traded security. But the two organizations were worlds apart. LOR was a team of gifted academics who had set out to bring a security to market for the first time. They had limited resources in terms of both financial and human capital. The Amex, on the other hand, had a developed network of traders and institutions they had done business with. They had a nose for sensing what the market wanted and a history of introducing new securities to the market. With the CIP product, they had also shown that they were fast learners and could build on an existing or proposed product. And although the Amex did not have deep pockets, they had more resources than their counterparts from the Bay Area.

Like LOR, the Amex chose the S&P 500 as the basis for its S&P depositary receipt—SPDR—vehicle. The S&P was a favorite of institutions, a huge pool of capital that essentially guaranteed liquidity. However, unlike LOR, the Amex opted not to use two separate security types. Instead, the Amex would utilize a single security type and would rely on exemptions from the SEC when they needed to diverge from the UIT's parameters. The Spider was much simpler than the SuperTrust products, making the concept easier to grasp and market.

The stakes in this venture couldn't have been higher. The Amex needed a grand slam—they called it a "big wave"—that would save the exchange from bleeding to death.[1] Revenue and listings had been dwindling for years. Newspapers that had always published the previous day's trading data were threatening to drop Amex's shrinking list from their pages.

Profit margins were under pressure, too. The Securities Act Amendments of 1975 had done away with fixed commissions, opening the door for discount brokers such as Charles Schwab. Traditional brokers had had to reduce their fees to stay competitive. That, in turn, had dragged down the profit margins of the exchanges. The NYSE had become more aggressive about courting and poaching Amex-listed stocks.

In order for the security to achieve the ambitious goals the Amex team had for it, it had to stay more stable than the closed-end fund shares that fluctuated above and below "fair value" prices. It needed to trade on an exchange at a price that was very close or exactly equal to the underlying net asset value of the index—in real time.

The Spider also had to be cost efficient. To minimize transaction expenses, the team decided on issuing units consisting of lots of fifty thousand or more shares.[2] This limited the scope and frequency of creations and redemptions. Only a specialist deemed an authorized participant could execute trades, a feature of the product that Riley attributed to Nathan Most.[3]

The price of the Spider shares was $100.[4] This reflected the Amex's understanding of what the market wanted: a too-expensive security was too expensive for retail investors to trade. Since the Spider allowed the physical delivery of stocks to the APs, they could conduct like-kind exchanges to create Spider units and avoid triggering a taxable event. Taxes, therefore, could be deferred until the investors sold their shares of the ETF. This exchange feature provided opportunities for automated arbitrage in the event that the underlying stocks or the fund shares became overpriced, thus ensuring the price of the fund shares would not stray far from the underlying securities' value.

Although the Amex wanted the Spider to appeal to retail investors, they understood that the majority of initial investors would be institutions. This meant the Spider would have tighter bid-ask spreads. Therefore, they set the Spider's expense ratio to be equal to Vanguard's S&P 500 mutual fund to compete directly with the fund at twenty basis points.

The Amex's goals for the Spider were ambitious. In inflation-adjusted figures, the Spider would need about $600 million in assets to break even and begin generating revenue.[5] At $600 million, the annual overhead of nearly $1.2 million seems manageable today, but in 1992, the Amex was making a huge commitment to develop, make viable, and survive the regulatory review of an experimental, unfamiliar, untested product aimed at a market of sophisticated, wary, conservative fund managers. At the same time, LOR's SuperShares basket product, the precursor of the Spider, was going down the tubes.

It was a Hail Mary pass for the Amex—a gamble requiring that the entire Amex board be in agreement with the launch. Burton Malkiel is credited with persuading his fellow board members to take a "necessary and calculated risk."[6] The board concurred and set aside funds to cover development of the Spider, legal expenses associated with getting it through the SEC, marketing and educating investors, and other costs until the Spider could pay its own way. But without a "big wave," everyone knew the Amex's future would be back where it all began: on the street.

18

Assembling a Team

The Securities and Exchange Commission held the key to the SPDR's success. Ivers Riley, "Mr. Put," had plenty of experience dealing with the SEC. But even for a seasoned expert, the task would be like herding cats. Riley recalled, "We were breaking regulatory ground. For the first time for an exchange, we would have to deal with all of the major divisions of the SEC simultaneously."[1] Fortunately for Riley and the Amex, LOR had done some of the heavy plowing.

Riley arranged a sit-down with SEC chairman Richard Breeden to see what could be done to limit the amount of red tape.[2] After Riley described the Spider, Breeden first said he hated the name and then said he was enthused about the concept. Within two weeks—a turnaround unheard of for a huge federal bureaucracy—Breeden had set up a meeting between himself, the Amex team, and the directors of each of the SEC's three principal divisions: Market Regulation (now Trading and Markets), Corporate Finance, and Investment Management.

Breeden's ardor had evolved into a mission. He presented the Amex proposal to his directors as something important to the stability of the markets, particularly in light of Black Monday. He wanted its review prioritized—completed in two weeks.[3] Riley and his colleagues returned to New York ebullient, convinced the Spider could launch almost as soon as the Amex formally submitted the application, which it did in June 1990.

Riley, Most, and Bloom were confident they had designed a winning product. Now they needed a winning infrastructure—cutting-edge technology, reliable execution, efficient custody, and robust back-office systems. Through working at an exchange, they had seen all the things that could go wrong behind the scenes. They needed a bank that, in addition to funds management and lending, could maintain records, could serve as the trustee of the "securities warehouse," and had demonstrated expertise in indexing.[4]

There was only one bank in the country that could fit the bill: State Street Bank, a two-hundred-year-old financial-services and bank-holding company in Boston. State Street counted among its past customers the very first mutual fund: Massachusetts Investors Trust, founded in 1924. The bank had created a niche for itself managing the plumbing of the mutual fund business: the physical transfer and custody of assets; transaction processing; and all the rest of the machinery that's required to keep an economic system functioning smoothly and reliably. State Street was a good fit for the Spider.

The bank was just as hungry and motivated as the Amex. State Street also needed a big wave. Competition had been heating up, and expensive technology was disrupting the old ways. Profit margins had been shrinking in what had been its bread-and-butter business. Just as the Amex was submitting its SPDR filing with the SEC, State Street was taking the bold step of recruiting a new CEO that, on paper, seemed out of its league—a leading industry executive with an entrepreneurial streak.

Marshall N. Carter, a West Pointer and decorated veteran of the Vietnam War, had worked at Chase Manhattan—many times bigger than State Street—for fifteen years. Carter had earned his stripes helping Chase build the nation's top global custody business. He was thought to be in line to become the bank's next CEO.

But Chase had its own problems. It had been struggling for several years in a market that had been invaded in the 1980s and become dominated by Japanese megabanks flush with capital from the tech boom and soaring auto exports. Since the economy tanked in 1989, Chase had been trying to dig itself out of a rut before it could be taken over by one of its stronger competitors. The bank had been aggressively cutting costs.

Marsh Carter was a builder, not a bean counter. When he tried to persuade Chase to invest $25 million in new systems and technology, he was told, "We're not in the information business."[5] At State Street, he'd be running his own show and would be able to build the tech- and data-driven banking business he envisioned.

Carter developed a process capable of tracking and annotating all the 401(k) data for clients, from handwork to computers.[6] This data could then be printed for easy access. The bank dubbed it the "Camera-Ready 401(k)," and the new access proved to be profitable for State Street and a big hit with their clients.

Carter saw the potential of Amex's Spider product. When the two agreed to work together, Carter authorized a Spider-dedicated team at State Street that wasted no time setting up the system needed to support it.

Carter picked Katherine C. Cuocolo to be his lieutenant and head up the State Street Spider support team. While Carter's pedigree was evident, Cuocolo's was anything but. The daughter of first-generation Italian immigrants, Cuocolo had worked her way up, beginning with a degree from UMass because it was a state school she could reach by bus.[7] But the Spider was a cutting-edge product, and women on the edge would often find their opportunities for leadership in new ventures. Cuocolo looked forward to the challenge.

Cuocolo's team, which would eventually grow to six hundred members, started with just one. State Street employees were willing to become involved—including James E. Ross, now the bank's chair of SPDR global business, who asked, "What are they working on?" shortly before the security's launch.[8]

State Street had to bear with the Spider team. Contrary to the development team's hopes and the security's early promise, the Spider was not passing quickly through SEC review. The delays added up to two or so years, and the expenses of maintaining the Spider team mounted. Most banks would have pulled the plug within the first year. Around State Street's executive suite, people outside the Spider bubble began asking themselves and each other, "Why are we spending all these millions on a second-rate exchange?" But Carter—like Riley, Most, Bloom, Malkiel, Breeden, and all the others—was on a mission.

State Street's role as custodian of the assets in the Spider UIT, record keeper, and entity responsible for the delivery of securities in a cashless transaction presented a unique challenge. The Toronto team had created new TIPs units, but this occurred quarterly. The Spider, on the other hand, could be created (or redeemed) any time the necessary stocks were available on any trading day. The Spider required robust and reliable accounting and custody systems, record keeping that would not be triggered by a sales transaction, and coordinating the continual issuance of new securities while they were trading.[9]

When you connect the dots, it's clear that the Spider that launched the ETF as an institution would never have worked without State Street's eager embrace of new methods and technologies. The Amex had neither the resources nor the expertise to do it in house. Most had come upon a brilliant idea with the creation/redemption process. But for his brilliant idea to work, a system was needed that would record the *exchange* of creation units in the ETF for the five hundred underlying stocks that comprised the S&P 500. Until State Street's team, no such mechanism existed; continuous net settlement (CNS), the settlement system used at the Amex and the other exchanges to process their stock trades, could only transfer shares against cash payments.

But the increase in trade volume had put even greater emphasis on accurately maintaining records of who owned what, and the National Securities Clearing Corporation (NSCC)—a joint creation of the Amex, the NYSE, and the NASDAQ, established to maintain these records—could see what State Street aimed to do for the Spider. Dave Kelly, CEO of the NSCC, joined the growing crowd of believers and won his board's support to modify NSCC's system to accommodate the Spider's cashless transfers.

NSCC developed the creation/redemption mechanism conceived by Most and conducted tests that involved State

Street and the market specialists who would be responsible for submitting the creation/redemption orders. With all the kinks they could find ironed out, the Spider was ready to trade on the exchange.

With so many advocates, it may seem strange that the Amex was still waiting for approval two or so years after SEC chairman Richard Breeden told his directors to turn around the Spider's review in two weeks. But the overseers of the review would not be coaxed by presidential appointee Breeden. As the review process dragged on, the Spider still had not brought in any revenue. It was in danger of becoming a money pit for the already-beleaguered Amex and State Street.

There was also a fear that competitors, with years to parse the Amex application, would come up with something better. The Amex could only watch with envy as the Toronto Exchange waltzed through the approval process with Canadian regulators and issued its basket product, the TIPs. The Amex team and its Spider partners and missionaries fell into a funk. Would the Spider ever become the viable saving grace they needed it to be?

19

The Spiderwoman

In the 1990s, before its move to Fifth Street adjacent to Union Station, the Securities and Exchange Commission headquarters building was a nondescript, rectangular building as interesting as a file cabinet. The drab exterior belied the drama unfolding inside.

The Spider application was running a gauntlet through a bureaucratic maze of regulations issued by three different divisions within the SEC, each with its own sense of purpose and authority. The trinity of statutes governing the issuance of new securities consisted of the Securities Act of 1933, the Securities Exchange Act of 1934, and the Investment Company Act of 1940. These laws were passed in the aftermath of the Crash of 1929 and during the ensuing Great Depression as the federal government wrested regulation of the markets from the states. Winning approval for the Spider had turned from a hopeful sprint into a marathon and, finally, into a legal slog.

There were no attorneys with experience in what would become known as ETFs. Riley and Most ended up working with Kathleen Moriarty from Orrick, Herrington & Sutcliffe, a San Francisco–based firm that specialized in technology and the financial sector.

Moriarty, like so many people associated with the birth and growth of ETFs, had a somewhat hybridized career. She had studied psychology and opened a practice in Washington for a couple of years before deciding to pursue a law degree, which she earned at Notre Dame. She would eventually become known throughout the ETF industry as Spiderwoman for her role in the development of the Spider and many other funds.

In the summer between her second and third years of law school, Moriarty had divided her clerkship between conducting research for First Amendment cases and preparing the prospectuses for municipal bonds. Although upon beginning the clerkship Moriarty did not know what a municipal bond was, when her first assignment was to research whether or not the World Trade Center could be sold, her interest was piqued. She found the municipal bond work far more interesting, worked on hospital bonds for a time, and then was assigned to work on unit trusts issued by Paine Webber.

The unexpected departure of a senior partner made Moriarty the point person on the Paine Webber account— before she had even taken, let alone passed, the bar exam. Her banishment to what was then considered the hinterlands of unit trusts turned out to be perfect for her interests and temperament.

Although still a junior partner at Orrick, she became the attorney to whom the Amex entrusted its most important project: guiding the Spider through the regulatory minefield. In the end, it was the vaguest and least precise regulation that helped the Amex the most—a provision that speaks to the foresight of those who drafted it half a century earlier. Times change, systems evolve, and exemptions to certain requirements should be an option. Section 6(c) of the Investment Company Act states:

> The Commission by rules and regulations upon its own motion, or by order upon application, may conditionally or unconditionally exempt any person, security, or transaction, or any class or classes of persons, securities, or transactions, from any provision or provisions of this title or of any rule or regulation thereunder, if and to the extent that such exemption is necessary or appropriate in the public interest and consistent with the protection of investors and the purposes fairly intended by the policy and provisions of this title.

The securities available to investors in 1990 were the same ones defined in the Securities Act of 1933—closed-end funds, mutual funds, and a UIT. Moriarty repeatedly and successfully invoked the "necessary and appropriate in the public interest" clause for the Spider.

The Spider was proposed to be a perpetual IPO while simultaneously trading on the market. Conceptually, the creation/redemption process was the equivalent of a stock's IPO. The specialist selling shares to brokers was the secondary market, and the specialist came to be referred to as the AP.

Attorneys at the SEC wondered whether an AP would become an underwriter during some of his or her activities. This alone would have grounded the Spider's launch, because for a specialist to be deemed an underwriter, they would be required to conduct due diligence on all five hundred stocks underlying the Spider—which would be impossible.

After the Spider had been mired for some time in the morass of the SEC bureaucracy, Chairman Breeden intervened. He called for a meeting at the SEC headquarters. When Moriarty, the Amex team, and others arrived, they were ushered into a large hall reserved for formal public events. Riley recalled later, "Upon entry, we were confronted by an arrangement of tables seating dozens of the leading players from each of the three divisions and the General Counsel's office. This would have been precedent-setting and intimidating enough, but in the background came the icing on the cake. THEY HAD SET UP BLEACHERS, seating all the young attorneys from each division. I fully expected to see lions released before we left the room."[1]

Despite the intimidating appearance of the meeting, Moriarty and the legal team at the American Stock Exchange did their job well, and the Spider was finally able to move forward when the Amex agreed to bring on brokers to serve as nonfunctioning underwriters. Riley commented, "Voilà! Approval."[2]

20

From Spears to Spiders

The security we now know as the Spider was initially referred to as the SPIR—the S&P index receipt. The Amex's Steven Bloom recalls this was quickly nixed because "we didn't like the imagery of spears being thrown around the floor."[1] Bloom is credited with the suggestion to substitute *depositary receipts* for *index*, resulting in SPDR. (The official name is the SPDR Trust, Series 1.)[2] Riley recalled that the choice served "to avoid at all costs waving any red flags in the face of the mutual fund industry" and to avoid drifting onto the radar of the futures industry.[3]

The next step in the branding process was to come up with a memorable stock symbol. Spider did not lend itself easily to a ticker. The S&P 500 Index had already claimed SPX, and SPI was also unavailable. The marketing department liked the appeal of SXY, but this was rejected as sounding too risqué. Instead, pivoting from SPI, the final choice was the now-familiar SPY.[4]

As 1992 wore on and the time to launch approached, the Amex team continued to work on the endless details involved in debuting a new product. There were dry trading runs to test the system, and these appeared to go without a hitch. The Amex lined up specialists to handle the creation units and briefed the floor members on trading. At State Street in Boston, Cuocolo's team conducted a lot of end-to-end testing to make sure things would run smoothly. Most, who was always very interested in every aspect of any project (his favorite magazine was *Scientific American,* according to his daughter), met with the various parties. He and Moriarty became good friends, and their collaboration is worth noting. For years, Jews and Catholics—not always welcome at the other exchanges—had worked together at the Amex. Now an Eastern European Jew (Most) was working together with an Irish Catholic (Moriarty) on a security they hoped would save the exchange.

Launch day was near, but as the day approached, Gary Eisenreich, a specialist with Spear, Leeds & Kellogg, realized that the Spider was lacking an essential exemption to allow short selling of the Spider on a downtick.[5] Before the Crash of 1929, traders could sell short on a downtick, using the short-sell technique (selling borrowed securities to buy them back later upon speculation that the price would fall) to add downward pressure to stocks and make a profit at the expense of the market. The uptick rule halted this abuse by allowing short selling only when the stock price was either stable or rising (an uptick).

As Eisenreich knew, however, an AP has to create new units when the demand for new shares exists, whether the market is rising or falling. Whenever APs create units, they need to hedge their position. Otherwise, an AP would not create shares. Without an exception to the uptick rule, the Spider APs would be disinclined to create new shares.

Eisenreich made the call just in time. Together with Moriarty, the two of them worked with the SEC to build an uptick rule exemption for the Spider—a provision that proved essential to the Spider's success.

— 21 —

Launch

After a meticulous development, the Spider team had things in place for the launch. The initial seeding of the trust occurred on January 22, 1993, with Spear Leeds putting up the initial $11.5 million (adjusted for inflation)—enough for the creation of three units of fifty thousand shares each. LOR had launched their ill-fated SuperTrust just three months earlier with initial subscriptions of nearly $2 billion. The Spider started out smaller, but it was the first stand-alone ETF to trade on a US stock exchange, a distinction that in the long run would make all the difference.

To announce the Spider's arrival, the Amex ran a full-page ad in the *Wall Street Journal*, hung a huge black spider prop over the trading floor, and populated the exchange with all sorts of spider-themed gewgaws, including smaller rubber spiders, spider rings, and spider T-shirts, which are sought-after souvenirs today.[1] State Street's Marsh Carter had the honor of ringing the exchange's opening bell, and the Spider was officially born. The first recorded trade was for 3,100 shares at a price of 43 31/32.[2] By the time the closing bell rang that first day, the Spider had traded more than 1,000,000 shares, and the exchange floor's usual litter of trade tickets included many of the spider rings and toys, which were swept up with the trash and discarded. But despite all the excitement, Kathleen Moriarty looked out at the exchange trading floor at the end of that first day and sensed that it would take a lot of time and effort to win widespread interest. She realized that there were only about a hundred people who actually knew what a Spider was.[3] The compensation the Spider offered brokers was about a quarter what they earned selling other unit trusts. Steven Bloom recalled, "We couldn't get anybody to sell it."[4] The Spider's growth would not come from brokers looking for some fat trades.

The Spider was generating more volume on the exchange and some additional revenue for brokers, but it was a long way from the (adjusted) $600 million of assets needed to break even. Still, by trading on the Amex, the Spider had taken trading volume away from the NYSE, something the Curb rarely got to do.

Over the winter months and into the spring, assets trickled in, but trading of the Spiders was sluggish, hitting a low of only 17,900 shares on June 10.[5] The disparity between assets increasing while trading volume remained low suggested the Spider was being used primarily for buy-and-hold strategies—not a source of recurring revenue.

Brokers on the floor weren't excited about trading a security that wasn't generating much interest.

The first real breakthrough came at the end of June, when Daiwa Securities took a $90 million position, bringing the total assets to the $300 million break-even point.[6] By the end of 1993, the Spider had accumulated $461 million in assets.[7] It was clear that if the Spider were to provide the revenue sufficient to save the Amex, it would have to come from trading volume, which would depend in part on the enthusiasm of specialists like Todd Hollander of Susquehanna and Gary Eisenreich of Spear, Leeds & Kellogg, who had spotted the short-sale/uptick issue. Eisenreich set a goal of one million shares a day. To get there, he employed what he called the "cocktail investing" strategy. He talked about Spiders in all his social interactions, telling people he'd invested in them and how great they were. Some of those people would go home and call their brokers to get them in on the hot new investment vehicle they'd just heard about at a cocktail party. Then those people would brag at their next cocktail party that they'd bought Spiders. And so on. Volume inched up in the spring, and by summer, Eisenreich had reached his goal and was setting new ones.

Eisenreich also did what he could to accommodate trades to make buying and selling the Spider easier. Trading a basket security that required an actual basket of stocks as collateral was a unique challenge before data automation became so sophisticated, particularly when a trade amount would allow full shares in each S&P 500 stock. Eisenreich created a spreadsheet that calculated the number of shares in the underlying stocks for a given trade, with a cell colored yellow for his plug number. He called the yellow cell "the gizmo." To make trading the Spider easier, he freely gave out his spreadsheet, which was quite advanced for its time, to brokers and traders. Its embedded formulas caught on with other brokers and traders. Today, everything we do online starts with a gizmo—the input field—but in 1993, floor traders were still using handheld calculators and pencils.

22

Expanding Horizons

First to market in the race for the ultimate basket security was Toronto's TIPs. Second was LOR's SuperTrust. Third was the Amex team's Spider. The fourth product launched—within six months of two others—was Morgan Stanley's optimized portfolios as listed securities (OPALS), a proprietary debt instrument that would be limited to its extensive global customer base. The biggest challenge for the OPALS was managing cross-border taxation and regulation. In fact, the product appeared abroad before it was available in the US.

Morgan Stanley debuted the OPALS in April 1993, three months after the Spider, and it took off quickly, becoming especially popular in Asia and the Pacific.[1] By the end of the first year, the OPALS had gathered about $17 billion in assets (adjusted for inflation), on which Morgan Stanley was earning almost eighty-five basis points—or about $150 million.[2] Eventually, Morgan Stanley would have at least ninety OPALS products.

Robert Tull, the Morgan Stanley executive who had headed up the firm's new order-execution system just in time for Black Monday, now had two feathers in his cap. Yet even as Tull basked in the glow of his success, he saw further potential in the structure of the Spider and began exploring how the OPALS might be repackaged as an exchange-traded fund, particularly one that would appeal to its large global customer base.

A UIT like the Spider, with securities from exchanges around the world, would be unwieldy at best, and the SEC would not allow it. Morgan Stanley would need to structure its product as a mutual fund that could lend shares, reinvest dividends, and invest cash—revenue-generating activities prohibited to a UIT. Morgan Stanley's approach required its own set of SEC exemptions on top of the many that had been granted for the Spider and SuperTrusts.

The final product, after much tinkering, needed a moniker that would do for Morgan Stanley what Spider and SPY had done for the Amex. The name they chose for their international basket security was "world equity benchmark series"—WEBS. It was a marketing gimmick that paid tribute to the Spider. In the process of outsourcing most of what they had done in house for the OPALS, the firm recruited Gary Eisenreich at the Amex to do for the WEBS what he'd done for the Spider.

Unlike the Spider, WEBS required an investment manager for their funds. Morgan Stanley chose Wells Fargo Investment Advisors, a natural fit given the strong relationship Morgan Stanley had with the firm. It was Morgan Stanley's brand-new system that had successfully executed Wells Fargo's trades on Black Monday. Furthermore, Wells had been a pioneer in index-based investing, credited with having created the first index fund in 1971, and had been a mainstay ever since.

As the Spider continued to grow and Morgan Stanley's OPALS and related products proved durable, other institutions began developing and issuing ETFs. Deutsche Bank rolled out its international suite of products, called country baskets, the brainchild of Joseph A. LaCorte and Herbert D. Blank, which became the first ETFs to trade on the NYSE. In 1996, Morgan Stanley launched the WEBS, seventeen ETFs on the Amex. The launch festivities included a private lunch at the St. Regis Hotel with Henry Kissinger as the keynote speaker. Morgan Stanley gave out swag at six exchanges around the globe and then anxiously waited for the trades to come in.

Trades for WEBS came in dribs and drabs—modest orders because none of the wire houses understood the product yet. But the launch went off without a hitch.

By January of 1997, WEBS had accumulated $250 million in assets to the country baskets' $240 million.[3] Although the assets under management had a similar value, on the trading end, WEBS was generating thirteen times more volume than country baskets.[4] Morgan

Stanley's product had the advantage of being a hedging tool for traders with positions in OPALS. The country baskets failed to generate much interest from traders and were not embraced within Deutsche Bank, where active management was the de rigueur. Deutsche Bank put the fund up for sale. Standard & Poor's turned it down, and then so did State Street. Insiders took to referring to the fund as "country caskets."[5] Deutsche finally closed the fund, leaving the WEBS as the only international equities ETF.

Morgan Stanley had demonstrated that the market had a growing appetite for ETFs, an appeal that extended outside of the US. Though the funds themselves had had a mixed reception, it was clear that the ETF's versatility could reach international markets, not just large segments of the domestic market.

By 1996, Nathan Most was well into his eighties. He retired from the Amex at the urging of his wife, Evelyn, but the Amex had been able to build on the products he and Bloom had made possible, launching the S&P MidCap (MDY), sponsored by Merrill Lynch, in 1995. A third progeny, the DIAMONDS Trust (for *D*ow *J*ones *I*ndustrial *A*verage *Mo*del *N*ew *D*epository *S*hares), launched on the Amex floor on January 20, 1998. In December 1998, State Street Global Advisors launched its Select SPDR, allowing an investor to purchase a basket comprising the stocks in just one of the sectors of the S&P 500.

As ETFs proliferated, the concept developed. Later funds chose the mutual funds as an underlying investment vehicle for the ETF. Deutsche Bank and Morgan Stanley did so out of necessity for their funds, but it became clear that a UIT was much more rigid; it did not allow for security lending or reinvesting dividends. Both WEBS and country baskets, as well as Select SPDRs, were optimized. The mutual fund platform allowed the ETFs to not only engage in security lending and reinvest dividends but also employ swaps and options. In addition, serving as a mutual fund's investment manager generated revenues more substantial than sponsoring an ETF. State Street was the first to grasp this nuance. When they comprehended the full potential of ETFs, they became dominant players in the industry. As more and more ETFs showed up, it became clear just how versatile the vehicle was—able to represent an index, an entire country, or a market segment.

The Amex had really hit on something with the Spider, and it did serve as a "wave" for the exchange. Volume grew, and assets hit the $1 billion mark three years after launch.[6] But the wave wasn't big enough. At the time, the Nasdaq listed about 5,400 companies with a total market cap of $1.8 trillion. The NYSE had 3,000 listing companies with a market cap of $11.8 trillion. The Amex listed only 783 companies, worth just $168 billion. Their Hail Mary pass had been completed, but it came up short of the necessary score.

Throughout the exchange's history, from the Curb to toy spiders, the Amex had lagged in technology, and they were falling further behind. The DIAMONDS proved to be a last hurrah for the Amex as an independent exchange. In March 1998, the board agreed to be acquired by the Nasdaq. The sale included a commitment by the Nasdaq to invest $110 million in technology to make the Amex competitive.[7]

On November 2, 1998, when the merger was completed, the National Association of Securities Dealers (NASD) released a statement proclaiming, "This combination creates the world's first financial market that brings together central auction specialists and multiple Market Maker systems"—floor brokers and computerized terminals.[8] But the experiment—to mix both the cultures and the systems of the two exchanges—proved unworkable. The firms later parted, and the Amex became independent again, albeit for only a short while. They finally succumbed to the NYSE, closing their doors at 86 Trinity for the last time on December 1, 2008.

Regardless of the plight of its creators, the Spider and other ETFs continued to grow. After a brief outburst of new fund issues, the pace slowed down considerably. The next significant ETF was the Nasdaq 100 (QQQ). Launched in 1999, it represented the hundred largest nonfinancial stocks comprising the Nasdaq. Most were technology stocks that had been hugely popular as the internet—and everything related to it—became essential tools of modern life. It wasn't groundbreaking in its design or the assets it held but in the interest and excitement it brought to ETFs. Everyone wanted in on technology.

The QQQ, called the cube, broke every trading record as it rode the final leg of the internet boom. A year after its launch, it boasted $6 billion in assets alone. The rest of the industry had $33.8 billion. But then the Nasdaq peaked on March 10, 2000, one year after the fund's launch. The dot-com bubble burst, and the cube lost most of its volume. Still, it introduced a whole new generation of investors and investors to ETFs.

Assets continued to grow, and new investors discovered ETFs, but a couple of issuers were questioning whether to be in the business. Although the WEBS had gathered more than $800 million in assets, Morgan Stanley found that sponsoring ETFs was not nearly as profitable as issuing OPALs had been.[9] The industry was evolving. With Bob Tull having left Morgan Stanley on the eve of the WEBS' launch, they lacked a strong advocate in the firm, which began looking to exit the industry.

23

ETFs for Everyone

The Toronto Exchange's TIPs and the Amex's Spider had thrown open the door for exchange-traded funds. Morgan Stanley's WEBS and Deutsche Bank's country baskets advanced ETFs by proving that they could be used in a family of funds; they were versatile, and issuers began applying them to new assets and strategies. WEBS and baskets also showed that the mutual fund structure was superior to the UIT in most cases. The opportunities for ETFs were expanding, but the hurdle of how to effectively reach the retail investor remained. Each of the ETF issuers had coveted the retail business, but so far, they had been unable to effectively exploit that market.

Wells Fargo, which had blazed the trail in indexing in the seventies, would reappear in the story to blaze the trail to the retail investor—or, at least, the team that had originated with the San Francisco bank would. Wells Fargo sold their stake in WFIA to Barclays PLC, making a strategic decision to focus on banking.[1] Barclays, a venerable British banking firm looking to expand across the Atlantic, then merged WFIA with their own asset management group, creating Barclays Global Investors (BGI). Grauer was still at the helm, but the reins were soon given over to Patricia (Patti) C. Dunn, a lifelong bank employee who had risen from the firm's secretarial typing pool to eventually lead BGI.

Barclays, much like the other banks, was considering what opportunities would arise from the impending repeal of Glass-Steagall, the legislation that had thwarted McQuown and his team's Stagecoach fund a decade and a half earlier. Their chief investment officer, Lawrence G. Tint (creator of horizon funds, which we know as target date funds), proposed ETFs, which were consistent with the firm "taking index investing to the retail investors." Grauer, Dunn, and the firm's leadership agreed that the retail market had remained virtually untouched because the prior entrants had not properly branded their offerings. But branding required capital and a salesforce, neither of which the bank possessed in any abundance, especially in the States.

Selling a new, retail-oriented ETF to the Barclays board was no small task, because Barclays / Wells Fargo had been involved in ETFs from their outset, and ETFs had not proven they could justify such a large branding campaign. When the board allocated $150 million to spend on what would become iShares, over the next three years, Barclays generated only about $100 million in net income each year.[2] The bet was placed not upon experience but upon the potential few others saw for ETFs. J. Parsons—who, after cutting his teeth on LOR's SuperTrust, came over to BGI in 1999 to head up the iShares sales team—noted that coworkers came to him and complained, "Patti is betting our bonus on this!"[3] But Parsons knew that if Barclays were to make waves in the US, it would be through the ETF.

Barclays' "bet" came on the heels of Deutsche Bank shutting down their country baskets (without selling them) and Morgan Stanley's surrender of WEBS' sponsorship. Firms were leaving the ETF industry. Barclays' contrarian strategy was to add a full palette of funds to the rebranded WEBS to create the iShares family of ETFs. Grauer noted that the Barclays team was elated to find the iShares name available. The San Francisco firm could not believe their good fortune. Apple had claimed virtually everything else with the *i* moniker. With a brand name, a vision, and a handful of funds, they began to develop their strategy.

Armed with a $150 million budget allegedly offset by $50 million provided by the American Stock Exchange for trading rights to iShares, Barclays moved forward. To head up this effort, Dunn broke with the Wells Fargo culture and gave the reins to Lee Kranefuss, an outsider who had worked with the firm as a consultant. Kranefuss was charged with making the bank's $100 million gamble pay off. But all of this might very easily not have happened at all.

The iShares team was confident that they could take market share from the large mutual fund companies. These same companies that had allowed index investing to develop under their noses were allowing the story to repeat with ETFs. The lone exception was the company that, to most folks, *was* index investing: Vanguard. With their broad client base and extensive network of brokers, Vanguard was keenly focused on the retail market and could pose a formidable threat. Had Barclays suspected that Vanguard intended to enter the ETF market, it is doubtful they would have made such a large commitment. iShares might have never happened.

24

What Might Have Been

At the time Barclays was preparing to launch iShares, the Vanguard Group had accumulated \$107 billion in assets.[1] Vanguard was not only *established* in mutual fund indexing; they were *entrenched*. Their license of Standard and Poor's 500 Index, capped at \$50,000 per year, has been referred to as the deal of the century. Similar licenses today would generate fees in the millions, not thousands.[2]

With such a strong commitment to indexing, many naturally assumed that Vanguard would issue their own ETFs. But Jack Bogle's attitude had remained unchanged since Most presented his idea a decade earlier. Bogle said, "The ETF is like the famous Purdey shotgun that's made over in England. It's great for big game hunting, and it's great for suicide. My problem then and now is that index funds are meant to be used for big-game hunting. And if I were trying to capture the market return over a lifetime, I'm going to do fine. But investors that are trading them all day, every day, they are making a terrible mistake. It will be suicidal to their investment capital."[3]

As went Bogle, so did Vanguard. But in the nineties, Bogle suffered heart problems that led him to step aside from his CEO role in 1996. Succeeding him was his hand-picked successor, John J. Brennan, who had been with the firm since the early eighties and was expected to maintain the course Bogle had set for the firm. But Brennan's CIO, George U. Sauter, strongly advocated for ETFs. He was supported by Joseph Rizzello, who had recently joined the firm from the Philadelphia Stock Exchange. Brennan finally gave the go-ahead, and Vanguard began preparing their foray into ETFs.

Vanguard may very well have filed their ETFs with the SEC before BGI filed the iShares. Their funds would be called Vipers, short for Vanguard index participation equity receipts, the name inspired by CIP, TIPs, and the SPDR. The Vanguard team debated whether to notify McGraw Hill (owner of Standard & Poor's) of their intention to use their indexes in three of their ETFs. After much debate, they decided not to notify the index owner—against the advice of Rizzello, who had encountered a similar situation at the Philadelphia Exchange. This misstep turned out to be lucky for the underdog iShares.

A month after Vanguard filed the Viper, Standard & Poor's filed suit in a New York district court to bar Vanguard from using the S&P indexes in ETFs.[4] Unbeknownst to Vanguard, S&P had reached an agreement with BGI to allow them exclusive use of their indexes in their iShares ETFs—far more lucrative to McGraw Hill. Vanguard retired to their Valley Forge offices to determine which route they would take. As the three affected indexes (the S&P 500, S&P 500 Growth, and the S&P 500 Value) were the centerpiece of their ETF strategy, Vanguard refrained from launching the other two funds as well.

Confident that their twenty-year agreement with the S&P 500 Index allowed them to use the indexes with their ETFs, Vanguard pursued the matter in the courts. Much to their disappointment, a federal district court judge ruled against Vanguard and in favor of S&P in the spring of 2001.[5] The indexing giant would have to look elsewhere. Vanguard issued only a single fund in 2001, the Vanguard total stock fund. The fund tracked the MSCI Broad Market Index and has proved to be quite a success. But this paled in comparison to iShares' forty ETFs issued the prior year. Not until 2004 would Vanguard release four more ETFs, but by then, iShares was the acknowledged market leader.

25

Cracking the Retail Market

In preparing iShares, Barclays had not only assembled a top-notch team within their ranks; they had also assembled a crackerjack team of advisors. LaCorte and Blank of country baskets served as advisors. Tint remained with Barclays for the first year of the iShares' development. But the backbone of iShares was the marketing and sales team. J. Parsons had gained valuable experience with the SuperTrust. LOR had raised a billion dollars for the fund, but the securities' infrequent trading reflected retail investors' unwillingness to embrace what was primarily an institutional fund. Wells Fargo / Barclays had worked on the SuperTrust, but the experience and operational knowledge gained from working with Morgan Stanley on the WEBS is what gave them confidence in the ETF structure for the iShares.

Barclays developed twin goals with iShares. First, establish the premier ETF in a range of market sectors, and lock up the premier benchmark in that segment, thus deterring competitors. Joe LaCorte likened the acquisition of all valuable intellectual property (S&P, Russell, MSCI, etc.) to having prime housing lots on the fairway of a golf course.[1] Second, invest heavily in marketing, as well as in education.[2] iShares would have a sales team trained to educate investors, especially RIAs, to use ETFs to execute any portfolio strategy. iShares were not a collection of standalone products but a full family of ETFs that allowed an investor to cover the entire market with only ETFs. iShares allowed ordinary investors to invest fully in the market in a way that, just ten years earlier, had been available only to the wealthy.

Barclays implemented two things that helped breed the success of iShares. First, Kranefuss separated the sales team from the rest of the bank. This allowed them to develop the culture that would be necessary for a sales-driven unit. Next, Parsons oversaw the rigorous training of the sales team, which included pulling the team of thirty men and women off of the road for two weeks.[3] Such intensive training and preparation is now standard in the industry, but the commitment Barclays made in terms of resources and personnel was groundbreaking at the time. They also employed road shows, much like the exchanges had. One veteran of the Barclays caravan was none other than Thomas Dorsey, who, in addition to promoting the iShares, worked with Barclays to become perhaps the first ETF strategist.

With commitment, strategy, and some serendipity, Barclays soon emerged as the leader in ETFs. The market had seen how versatile the funds were. Now they saw how well they could work for the retail investor.

In 2000, Barclays unveiled their iShares brand to investors and launched forty new ETFs. Their combined strategy of a retail focus and a well-trained sales team enabled the firm to gather a whopping $7 billion in assets by the end of 2000 and $17 billion by the end of 2001, despite a falling market.[4] But what many viewed as an overnight success had been years in the making.

Architects of the first ETFs continued to play a role as the funds advanced and evolved. Nathan Most not only lived to see the iShares launch but played an important role in their making. Patti Dunn had invited him to join and chair the iShares board. Likewise, Steven Bloom did much of the work in preparing Nasdaq's very successful cube for launch.

In 2002, when the SEC considered actively managed ETFs, Most submitted that while he did not oppose the idea of a security similar to the ETF representing a managed portfolio, he advised against using the term "exchange-traded fund" to represent anything other than a passively managed index to avoid confusion.[5] Time has borne out the wisdom of his advice.

Most remained active on the Barclays board, serving as one of the key advisors on ETFs, until November 2004. One day, he called to say he would be unable to attend the next board meeting. He had been battling congestive heart failure for some time, and he lost the battle on December 3 of that year.

The *New York Times* and the *Wall Street Journal* both noted the passing of Nathan Most.[6] The markets were beginning to grasp the magnitude of the work that Most, Bloom, Riley, and so many other teams had accomplished when they built the ETF.

The iShares proved to be a culmination of what had begun with McQuown, WFIA, and their index-focused investing almost thirty years earlier. With it, most of the innovation in the ETF's construction was complete. In its structure as well as in how it is marketed to investors, today's ETF can trace its roots to Barclays and then back to TIPs, Spiders, WEBS, and country baskets.

Today, ETF innovation is focused on the assets classes and the index construction underlying the funds. Most countries are represented by ETFs, some with multiple market caps. Asset classes that previously were reserved for the superwealthy are available to anyone with an online brokerage account—real estate, timber, water rights, metals, infrastructure, and, most recently, even marijuana. So too with investment strategies, as the hoi polloi can purchase ETFs that utilize puts and calls. With over five thousand ETFs on the market, ETFs have surpassed $5 trillion in assets under management.[7]

International players have found new ways to exercise the benefits of the ETF. Perhaps no other ETF has displayed the range of the security than the Hong Kong TraHKer, an ETF created by State Street for the central bank of Hong Kong in the late nineties to support their currency during the Asian financial crisis. Having acquired about 10 percent of the stocks trading on the Hang Seng, Hong Kong's central bank used the stocks in their ballooning portfolio to create ETFs. This enabled the central bank to divest their holdings in an orderly fashion without creating a major disruption in the markets and to execute this strategy without favoring (or harming) certain sectors. This was beyond the capability of any mutual fund or bond.

An ETF can be applied to most any asset, country, or investment strategy. This versatility is a big reason for its astounding success. When the markets collapsed on Black Monday, financial players saw the stock market, the futures market, the options market, and mutual funds all break down to a certain extent or at least reveal their weaknesses. No single security type could correct all the problems involved, but the ETF has improved each of these markets by making them more efficient, more robust, and, therefore, more liquid. They can be swapped and shorted, are used to manage risk and duration, and cover robotics and carbon credits. ETFs have even aided mutual fund investors, whether the investor uses ETFs or not, by driving down mutual fund expense ratios.

Twenty years ago, did Most, Bloom, and the other ETF architects foresee how far their brainchild would travel? Probably not. But in a stunning example of innovation and persistence, they pursued, designed, developed, and executed the elusive trade, and financial markets have never been the same.

Notes

INTRODUCTION

1. Sumit Roy, "2017 ETF Inflows Big Record Breaker," ETF.com, updated January 2, 2018, https://www.etf.com/sections/weekly-etf-flows/2017-etf-inflows-big-record-breaker.

2. Charles Schwab Corporation, "ETF Allure: Investors Have Nearly Doubled Allocations to ETFs in Five Years," news release, September 7, 2017, https://pressroom.aboutschwab.com/press-release/schwab-fundslaudus-funds-news/etf-allure-investors-have-nearly-doubled-allocations-etf.

3. State Street Global Advisors, *SPDR S&P 500 ETF Trust: A Unit Investment Trust*, September 30, 2018, 13, https://us.spdrs.com/public/SPDR%20SP%20500%20ETF%209.30.18%20Web%20Ready.pdf.

4. "SPY ETF Report: Ratings, Analysis, Quotes, Holdings," ETF.Com, https://www.etf.com/SPY#overview.

CHAPTER 1: WHEN MONEY MET MACHINE

1. "Stagecoach History," Wells Fargo History, Wells Fargo, https://www.wellsfargohistory.com/history/.

2. Peter L. Bernstein, *Capital Ideas: The Improbable Origins of Modern Wall Street* (Hoboken, NJ: Wiley, 2005), 27.

3. *Encylopaedia Britannica Online*, s.v. "S&P 500," https://www. britannica.com/topic/SandP-500.

4. Harry Markowitz, "Portfolio Selection," *Journal of Finance* 7, no. 1 (March 1952): 77–91.

5. Bernstein, *Capital Ideas*, 237.

6. Frederick Grauer, interview with the author, April 17, 2018.

7. Grauer.

8. Bernstein, *Capital Ideas*, 248.

9. John Andrew McQuown, interview with the author, August 9, 2018.

10. Grauer.

11. Martin E. Lybecker, "Bank-Sponsored Investment Management Services: Consideration of the Regulation Problems, and Suggested Legislative and Statutory Interpretive Responses," *Duke Law Journal* 1977, no. 5 (December 1977): 983.

12. Hugh F. Owens, "The SEC and Securities Markets— Some Current Developments" (address, Texas Group Investment Bankers Association of America, Dallas, TX, April 7, 1966), SEC.gov, https://www.sec.gov/news/ speech/1966/040766owens.pdf.

13. Investment Co. Inst. v. Camp, 401 U.S. 617 (1971).

14. McQuown.

15. David Beutel, "William Fouse: The Greatest Investor You've Never Heard Of," Portfolio Strategy, Seeking Alpha, April 17, 2013, https://seekingalpha.com/article/1349101-william-fouse-the-greatest-investor-youve-never-heard-of?page=1.

16. Beutel, "The Greatest Investor."

17. Grauer.

18. Brian Twomey, "The International Money Market," Managing Wealth, Investopedia, updated January 20, 2010, https://

www.investopedia.com/articles/forex/10/international-money-market.asp.

19. Joel Chernoff, "Barclays Global Investors Boss Takes a Powder: What Next for the Index King?," *InvestmentNews*, July 20, 1998, https://www.investmentnews.com/article/19980720/SUB/807200714/barclays-global-investors-boss-takes-a-powder-what-next-for-the-Indexing-King.

20. Grauer.

21. Chernoff, "Barclays Global Investors Boss Takes a Powder."

22. Grauer.

23. Douglas Frantz, "Wells Fargo Joins Venture to Crack Japanese Market," *Los Angeles Times*, June 28, 1989.

24. Barton Crockett, "Wells, Nikko Selling Money Manager to Barcclays PLC," *American Banker*, June 22, 1995, https://www.americanbanker.com/news/wells-nikko-selling-money-manager-to-barcclays-plc.

CHAPTER 2: THE ETF SPARK

1. Stuart Bruchey, *The Modernization of the American Stock Exchange 1971–1989* (New York: Garland Publishing, 1991), 35.

2. "Big Board Reports Fake Certificates," *New York Times*, August 10, 1971, https://www.nytimes.com/1971/08/10/archives/big-board-reports-fake-certificates.html.

3. "The Paper Jungle," *New York Times*, June 28, 1971, https://www.nytimes.com/1971/06/28/archives/the-paper-jungle.html.

4. "When Paper Paralyzed Wall Street: Remembering the 1960s Paperwork Crisis," FINRA, August 19, 2015, https://www.finra.org/investors/when-paper-paralyzed-wall-street-remembering-1960s-paperwork-crisis.

5. Frank Fabozzi, ed., *Handbook of Finance*, vol. 1, *Financial Markets and Instruments* (New York: Wiley, 2008).

6. Megan Groves, "The Birth of the Modern Stock Market," Cincinnati Stock Exchange, http://www.cincinnatistockexchange.us/the-birth-of-the-modern-stock-market-automation-and-impact/.

7. Investment Company Institute, "US Closed-End Funds," in *2018 Investment Company Fact Book: A Review of Trends and Activities in the Investment Company Industry*, http://www.icifactbook.org/ch5/18_fb_ch5.

8. "Total Net Assets of US-Registered Mutual Funds Worldwide from 1998 to 2017 (in Trillion U.S. Dollars)," Statista, 2018, https://www.statista.com/statistics/255518/mutual-fund-assets-held-by-investment-companies-in-the-united-states/.

Chapter 3: Black Monday

1. Lawrence J. De Maria, "Stocks Plunge 508 Points, a Drop of 22.6%; 604 Million Volume Nearly Doubles Record," *New York Times*, October 20, 1987, https://www.nytimes.com/1987/10/20/business/stocks-plunge-508-points-a-drop-of-22.6-604-million-volume-nearly-doubles-record.html.

2. Stan Hinden, "NASD Proposes Tougher OTC Trading Rules," *Washington Post*, November 17, 1987, https://www.washingtonpost.com/archive/business/1987/11/17/nasd-proposes-tougher-otc-trading-rules/3ab907b9-48ef-422a-9732-7669a0f22670/?noredirect&utm_term=.a20018ebac2c.

3. Floyd Norris, "A Computer Lesson Still Unlearned," High and Low Finance, *New York Times*, October 18, 2012, https://www.nytimes.com/2012/10/19/business/a-computer-lesson-from-1987-still-unlearned-by-wall-street.html.

4. Bruchey, *Modernization*, 144.

5. Bruchey, *Modernization*, 150.

6. Robert Tull, interview with the author, November 1, 15, 2017.

7. Tull.

8. Thomas Dorsey, interview with the author, August 23, 31, 2017.

9. "Milestones of the Dow Industrials," US News, CNBC, April 25, 2007, https://www.cnbc.com/id/18274839.

10. De Maria, "Stocks Plunge."

11. Dorsey.

12. De Maria, "Stocks Plunge."

13. "Best Time(s) of Day, Week & Month to Trade Stocks," Trading Strategy, Investopedia, updated October 29, 2018, https://www.investopedia.com/day-trading/best-time-day-week-month-trade-stocks/.

14. Andrew Feinberg, "Blown Away by Black Monday," *New York Times Magazine*, December 20, 1987, https://www.nytimes.com/1987/12/20/magazine/blown-away-by-black-monday.html.

15. Barry Nobel, interview with the author, July 21, 2017.

Chapter 4: Portfolio Uncertainty

1. Andrew Kupfer, "Leland, O'Brien, and Rubinstein: The Guys Who Gave Us Portfolio Insurance," *Fortune*, January 4, 1988, http://archive.fortune.com/magazines/fortune/fortune_archive/1988/01/04/70047/index.htm.

2. Hayne Leland, interview with the author, August 11, 2017.

3. Bernstein, *Capital Ideas*, 274.

4. Leland.

5. John O'Brien, interview with the author, May 29–31, 2018.

6. Bernstein, *Capital Ideas*, 282.

7. Leland.

8. Douglas Frantz, "Leland O'Brien's Image Marred in 'Meltdown': Pioneer Portfolio Insurers on the Defensive as Role in Market Skid Is Questioned," *Los Angeles Times*, November 2, 1987, http://articles.latimes.com/1987-11-02/business/fi-12069_1_portfolio-insurance.

9. Frantz, "Leland O'Brien's Image Marred."

10. Leland.

CHAPTER 5: TWO REPORTS

1. Thomas Klitgaard and James Narron, "Crisis Chronicles: The Long Depression and the Panic of 1873," *Liberty Street Economics* (blog), Federal Reserve Bank of New York, February 5, 2016, https://libertystreeteconomics.newyorkfed.org/2016/02/crisis-chronicles-the-long-depression-and-the-panic-of-1873.html.

2. Wikipedia, s.v. "Pecora Commission," updated September 5, 2018, https://en.wikipedia.org/wiki/Pecora_Commission.

3. *Report of the Presidential Task Force on Market Mechanisms: Submitted to the President of the United States, the Secretary of the Treasury, and the Chairman of the Federal Reserve Board* (Washington, DC: US Department of the Treasury, 1988).

4. "Flashback Wall Street: Black Monday," FINRA, October 14, 2016, http://www.finra.org/investors/flashback-wall-street-black-monday.

5. James Simpson, interview with the author, February 21, 2017.

6. *The October 1987 Market Break: A Report by the Division of Market Regulation US Securities and Exchange Commission* (Washington, DC: Securities and Exchange Commission, 1988), https://babel.hathitrust.org/cgi/pt?id=mdp.35128000946994;view=1up;seq=1.

7. *The October 1987 Market Break.*

8. Martin Mayer, "Suddenly, It's Chicago," *New York Times Magazine*, March 27, 1988, https://www.nytimes.com/1988/03/27/magazine/suddenly-it-s-chicago.html.

Chapter 6: An Extraordinary Man

1. Eric Balchunas, "Behind the ETF Revolution: How the US Government Inadvertently Launched an Industry," *Bloomberg Markets* 25, no. 1 (March 7, 2006).
2. *The October 1987 Market Break.*
3. Balchunas, "Behind the ETF Revolution."
4. Stephen Most, interview with the author, April 21, 2017.
5. Jim Wiandt, "Nate Most, Exchange-Traded Fund Inventor, Dies at Age 90," ETF.com, December 8, 2004, https://www.etf.com/sections/features/281.html?nopaging=1.
6. Jennifer Bayot, "Nathan Most Is Dead at 90; Investment Fund Innovator," *New York Times*, December 10, 2004, https://www.nytimes.com/2004/12/10/obituaries/nathan-most-is-dead-at-90-investment-fund-innovator.html.
7. Kathleen Pender, "Nathan Most, Creator of the Exchange-Traded Funds, Still a Visionary: He Foresees ETFs Rivaling, Even Replacing, Today's Mutual Funds," *San Francisco Chronicle*, July 18, 2000, https://www.sfgate.com/business/networth/article/Nathan-Most-Creator-of-Exchange-Traded-Funds-2713311.php.
8. Bayot, "Nathan Most Is Dead."
9. "In the Midst of Revolution: The SEC, 1973–1981," Securities and Exchange Commission Historical Society, http://www.sechistorical.org/museum/galleries/rev/rev02c.php.
10. Bruchey, *Modernization*, 75.
11. Bruchey, *Modernization*, 76.

Chapter 7: The Curb

1. Joseph A. Grundfest, "'Perestroika' on Wall Street: The Future of Securities Trading" (speech, Financial Executives Institute's 57th Annual Conference, San Francisco, CA, October 12, 1988), SEC.gov, https://www.sec.gov/news/speech/1988/101288grundfest.pdf.

2. Joseph Rizello, interview with the author, August 29, 2017.

3. Dominic Vitiello with George E. Thomas, *The Philadelphia Stock Exchange and the City It Made* (Philadelphia: University of Pennsylvania Press, 2010), 152–55.

4. Robert Sobel, *The Curbstone Brokers: The Origins of the American Stock Exchange* (New York: Macmillan, 1970), 12–13.

5. "Curb Bars Stocks Big Board Dropped: Securities Shut Out by Abolition of Unlisted Department Are Homeless Now," *New York Times*, April 2, 1910, https://www.nytimes.com/1910/04/02/archives/curb-bars-stocks-big-board-dropped-securities-shut-out-by-abolition.html.

6. Sobel, *Curbstone Brokers*, 88.

7. Sobel, *Curbstone Brokers,* 124–128.

8. Edwin C. Hill, "The Strangest Stock Market in the World: The Curb Market on Broad Street, a Unique New York Institution Which Is an Extraordinary Spectacle as Well as a Highly Important Financial Center," *Munsey's Magazine* 69 (February–May 1920): 46, https://books.google.com/books?id=BKPNAAAAMAAJ.

9. Bruchey, *Modernization*, 73.

10. Burton G. Malkiel, interview with the author, June 22, 2018.

11. Bruchey, *Modernization*, 116.

12. Jim Kharouf, "Ivers Riley: A Man for All Markets," John Lothian News, February 18, 2015, http://johnlothiannews.com/ivers-riley-man-markets/.

13. Kharouf, "Ivers Riley."

CHAPTER 8: A SPIDER IS BORN

1. Kharouf, "Ivers Riley."
2. Debbie Carlson, "Happy 25th Birthday: The SPY ETF Changed Investing," Funds, US News, January 18, 2018, https://money.usnews.com/investing/funds/articles/2018-01-18/happy-25th-birthday-the-spy-etf-changed-investing.
3. Wiandt, "Nate Most Dies at Age 90."
4. Burton G. Malkiel, interview with the author, June 22, 2018.
5. John Bogle, interview with the author, August 10, 2017.

CHAPTER 9: THE PHILADELPHIA FORAY

1. Vitiello with Thomas, *The Philadelphia Stock Exchange*, 26.
2. Vitiello with Thomas, *The Philadelphia Stock Exchange*, 156–59.
3. Vitiello with Thomas, *The Philadelphia Stock Exchange*, 159.
4. "Cboe History," Cboe, http://www.cboe.com/aboutcboe/history.
5. Vitiello with Thomas, *The Philadelphia Stock Exchange*, xxx.
6. Vitiello with Thomas, *The Philadelphia Stock Exchange*, 175.

CHAPTER 10: TURF WARS

1. John P. Caskey, "The Evolution of the Philadelphia Stock Exchange," *Federal Reserve Bank of Philadelphia Business Review* Q2 (2004): 18–29, https://www.philadelphiafed.org/-/media/research-and-data/publications/business-review/2004/q2/brq204jc2.pdf?la=en.
2. Vitiello with Thomas, *The Philadelphia Stock Exchange*, 119.
3. "Timeline of CME Achievements," CME Group, https://www.cmegroup.com/company/history/timeline-of-achievements.html.

4. "The Story of Futures Products," Stories of Financial Ingenuity and Innovation, CME Group, 2018, http://www.cmegroup. com/stories/index.html#!4-products-land.

5. Vitiello with Thomas, *The Philadelphia Stock Exchange*.

6. US Commodity Futures Trading Commission, Pub. L. No. 93-463, 88 Stat. (1974), GovInfo.gov, https://www.govinfo. gov/content/pkg/STATUTE-88/pdf/STATUTE-88-Pg1389. pdf.

7. Thomas A. Russo and Edwin Lyon, "The Exclusive Jurisdiction of the Commodity Futures Trading Commission," *Hofstra Law Review* 6, iss. 1 (1977): 57–91, Scholarly Commons at Hofstra Law, https://scholarlycommons.law.hofstra.edu/cgi/ viewcontent.cgi?article=1196&context=hlr.

8. Robert D. Hershey Jr., "Pact Opens New Kind of Futures," *New York Times,* December 8, 1981, https://www.nytimes. com/1981/12/08/business/pact-opens-new-kinds-of-futures. html.

9. "CFTC History in the 1980s," US Commodity Futures Trading Commission, https://www.cftc.gov/About/ HistoryoftheCFTC/history_1980s.html.

10. Kathleen Day, "The Derivatives Dilemma: Oversight Dispute Leaves Contracts in Perilous Limbo," *Washington Post*, 2000.

11. "Cboe History."

CHAPTER 11: PROBLEM SOLVERS AND TRAILBLAZERS

1. H. J. Maidenberg, "Futures/Options; OEX Trades: Early Signal," *New York Times*, March 12, 1984, https://www. nytimes.com/1984/03/12/business/futures-options-oex-trades-early-signal.html.

2. Nicholas Giordano, interview with the author, September 26, 2017.

3. Kurt Eichenwald, "Thomson Securities in Chapter 11," *New York Times*, March 29, 1990, https://www.nytimes.com/1990/03/29/business/thomson-securities-in-chapter-11.html.

4. Joseph Rizzello, interview with the author, June 20, 2017.

5. Since 2016, McGraw Hill has operated under the name S&P Global.

6. Rizzello.

CHAPTER 12: REGULATORS AND COMPETITORS

1. William Uchimoto, interview with the author, August 15–16, 2017.

2. Uchimoto.

3. John P. Caskey, "The Evolution of the Philadelphia Stock Exchange: 1964–2002" (working paper no. 03-21, Swarthmore College, Swarthmore, PA, 2003): 34, https://www.philadelphiafed.org/-/media/research-and-data/publications/working-papers/2003/wp03-21.pdf.

4. Uchimoto.

5. Uchimoto.

6. Lawrence Carrel, *ETFs for the Long Run: What They Are, How They Work, and Simple Strategies for Successful Long-Term Investing* (Hoboken, NJ: Wiley, 2008), 19.

7. Carrel, *ETFs for the Long Run*, 19.

8. Carrel, *ETFs for the Long Run*, 20.

9. Uchimoto.

10. Michael Freitag, "Key Ruling on 'Basket' Securities," *New York Times*, August 21, 1989, https://www.nytimes.com/1989/08/21/business/key-ruling-on-basket-securities.html.

11. Freitag, "Key Ruling."

12. Vitiello with Thomas, *The Philadelphia Stock Exchange*, 193.

CHAPTER 13: FORENSIC AFTERMATH

1. Kupfer, "Leland, O'Brien, and Rubinstein."

2. Kupfer, "Leland, O'Brien, and Rubinstein."

3. Hayne Leland, interview with the author, August 11, 2017.

4. Karl-Otto Hartmann to Brent J. Fields, Secretary, US Securities and Exchange Commission, August 16, 2015, SEC. gov, https://www.sec.gov/comments/s7-11-15/s71115-12.pdf.

5. Joshua Mendes and Andrew Evan Serwer, "This Exxon Stock Comes Custom-Blended," *Fortune*, May 12, 1986, http://archive.fortune.com/magazines/fortune/fortune_archive/1986/05/12/67526/index.htm.

6. Floyd Norris, "Market Place; Americus Trust Becoming Extinct," *New York Times*, February 13, 1992, https://www.nytimes.com/1992/02/13/business/market-place-americus-trust-becoming-extinct.html.

7. "The End of AT&T," Celtnet Telecommunications Companies, Celtnet.org, Wayback Machine Internet Archive, https://web.archive.org/web/20090112213916/http://www.celtnet.org.uk:80/telecos/AT&T-Bell-4.php.

8. Robert A. Jarrow and Maureen O'Hara, "Primes and Scores: An Essay on Market Imperfections," *Journal of Finance* 55, iss. 5 (December 1989): 1264, Wiley Online Library, https://onlinelibrary.wiley.com/doi/abs/10.1111/j.1540-6261.1989.tb02653.x.

9. Nils H. Hakansson, "The Purchasing Power Fund: A New Kind of Financial Intermediary," *Financial Analysts Journal* 32, no. 6 (November–December 1976): 49–59.

10. Joseph LaCorte, interview with the author, March 1, 2018.

11. Peter Tufano and Barbara B. Kyrillos, "Leland O'Brien Rubinstein Associates, Inc.: SuperTrust," *Harvard Business Review* (case study, June 6, 1994): 9.

12. Leland.

CHAPTER 14: THE CANADIAN COLLABORATION

1. K. Victor Chow, "An Economic Interpretation of the ETF Revolution: Suggestions for China ETF Innovation" (working paper, University of West Virginia, 2005): 16, http://www.sse.com.cn/aboutus/research/workstation/c/station20050930.pdf.
2. Andrew Clademenos, interview with the author, October 4, 2017.
3. Clademenos.
4. Clademenos.
5. Andrew Morgan, interview with the author, October 10, 2017.

CHAPTER 15: THE RACE TO MARKET

1. Cision, "Toronto Stock Exchange Celebrates 20 Years of Listing and Trading Exchange-Traded Funds," news release, April 22, 2010, https://www.newswire.ca/news-releases/toronto-stock-exchange-celebrates-20-years-of-listing-and-trading-exchangetraded-funds-539726331.html.
2. Andrew Morgan, interview with the author, October 10, 2017.
3. Andrew Clademenos, interview with the author, October 4, 2017.
4. Frances Denmark, "Happy 20th Birthday, ETFs: A Look Back at Nate Most and His Novel Idea," Portfolio, *Institutional Investor*, July 3, 2013, https://www.institutionalinvestor.com/article/b14zb9jjc7wzv1/happy-20th-birthday-etfs-a-look-back-at-nate-most-and-his-novel-idea#Frances+Denmark.
5. Robert Tull, interview with the author, November 1, 15, 2017.
6. Gary L. Gastineau, *The Exchange-Traded Funds Manual* (New York: Wiley, 2002): 151.
7. Tull.

8. Paul Aaronson, interview with the author, November 9, 2017.

Chapter 16: A Brilliant Failure

1. Ivers Riley, "ETF: The 'Hail Mary' Security," *Modern Trader* 34, no. 4 (March 2006), Questia, https://www.questia.com/magazine/1P3-995467691/etf-the-hail-mary-security.
2. John O'Brien, interview with the author, September 1, 2017.
3. Tufano and Kyrillos, "Leland O'Brien Rubinstein Associates, Inc."
4. Floyd Norris, "Market Place; New Securities Are a Hard Sell," *New York Times*, May 19, 1992, https://www.nytimes.com/1992/05/19/business/market-place-new-securities-are-a-hard-sell.html.

Chapter 17: The Hail Mary Security

1. Riley, "The 'Hail Mary' Security."
2. Riley, "The 'Hail Mary' Security."
3. Riley, "The 'Hail Mary' Security."
4. Frances Denmark, "Happy 20th Birthday, ETFs."
5. Riley, "The 'Hail Mary' Security."
6. Riley, "The 'Hail Mary' Security."

Chapter 18: Assembling a Team

1. Riley, "The 'Hail Mary' Security."
2. Riley, "The 'Hail Mary' Security."
3. Riley, "The 'Hail Mary' Security."
4. State Street Global Advisors, "SPY: The Idea That Spawned an Industry," SEC.gov, January 25, 2013, https://www.sec.gov/Archives/edgar/data/1222333/000119312513023294/d473476dfwp.htm.

5. Marsh Carter, interview with the author, January 30, 2018.

6. Carter.

7. Kathleen Cuocolo, interview with the author, October 30, 2017.

8. State Street Global Advisors, "SPY: The Idea."

9. Henry Belusa, interview with the author, December 12, 2017.

Chapter 19: The Spiderwoman

1. Riley, "The 'Hail Mary' Security."

2. Riley, "The 'Hail Mary' Security."

Chapter 20: From Spears to Spiders

1. State Street Global Advisors, "SPY: The Idea."

2. State Street Global Advisors, "SPY: The Idea."

3. Riley, "The 'Hail Mary' Security."

4. State Street Global Advisors, "SPY: The Idea."

5. Gary Eisenreich, interview with the author, January 18, 2018.

Chapter 21: Launch

1. Jerry Morgan, "Amex Weaves Intriguing Web with SPDRs," *Newsday, Buffalo News*, 1993.

2. Gary Eisenreich, interview with the author, January 18, 2018.

3. Kathleen Moriarty, interview with the author, January 5, 2018.

4. State Street Global Advisors, "SPY: The Idea."

5. State Street Global Advisors: "SPY: The Idea."

6. State Street Global Advisors: "SPY: The Idea."

7. Balchunas, "Behind the ETF Revolution."

Chapter 22: Expanding Horizons

1. Paul Aaronson, interview with the author, November 9, 2017.

2. Robert Tull, interview with the author, November 1, 15, 2017.

3. Carrel, *ETFs for the Long Run*, 32.
4. Carrel, *ETFs for the Long Run*, 32.
5. Carrel, *ETFs for the Long Run*, 32.
6. State Street Global Advisors, "SPY: The Idea."
7. Reuters, "Nasdaq to Pay $140 Million for Amex Merger," Business, *Wired*, March 18, 1998, https://www.wired.com/1998/03/nasdaq-to-pay-140-million-for-amex-merger/.
8. FINRA, "NASD and AMEX Merger Completed: The NASDAQ-AMEX Market Group Formed," news release, November 2, 1998, http://www.finra.org/newsroom/1998/nasd-and-amex-merger-completed-nasdaq-amex-market-group-formed.
9. Martine Costello, "Globetrotting with WEBS: World Equity Benchmark Shares (WEBS) Act Like Global Index Funds," Investing, CNN Money, June 10, 1998, https://money.cnn.com/1998/06/10/investing/q_webs/.

CHAPTER 23: ETFs FOR EVERYONE

1. Crockett, "Wells, Nikko Selling Money Manager."
2. Deborah Fuhr, "ETFs Are Busting Out All Over," ETF.com, January 1, 2001, https://www.etf.com/publications/journalofindexes/joi-articles/1251.html.
3. J. Parson, interview with the author, October 23, 2017.

CHAPTER 24: WHAT MIGHT HAVE BEEN

1. Michael Maiello, "2005 Mutual Fund Survey: The Un-Vanguard," *Forbes*, September 19, 2005, https://www.forbes.com/free_forbes/2005/0919/182.html.
2. Amy Baldwin, "Vanguard, S&P in Licensing Tussle," MarketWatch, September 5, 2001, https://www.marketwatch.com/story/vanguard-sp-in-dispute-over-500-use-2001-09-05.

3. Olivier Ludwig, "Bogle: ETF Trading Has No Social Value," ETF.com, September 29, 2011, https://www.etf.com/sections/features/9947-bogle-etf-trading-has-no-social-value.html.

4. "Standard & Poors Sues Vanguard Group," *Columbian*, June 9, 2000.

5. Jim Wiandt, "S&P Prevails—Vanguard Loses Landmark Lawsuit," Index Fund Advisors, April 26, 2001, https://www.ifa.com/articles/SP_PrevailsVanguard_Loses_Landmark_Lawsuit/.

CHAPTER 25: CRACKING THE RETAIL MARKET

1. Joseph LaCorte, interview with the author, March 1, 2018.

2. Fuhr, "ETFs Are Busting Out All Over."

3. J. Parson, interview with the author, October 23, 2017.

4. Carrel, *ETFs for the Long Run*, 45.

5. Nathan Most to Jonathan G. Katz, Secretary, US Securities and Exchange Commission, January 10, 2002, SEC.gov, https://www.sec.gov/rules/concept/s72001/s72001-13.pdf.

6. Jennifer Bayot, "Nathan Most Is Dead at 90; Investment Fund Innovator," *New York Times*, December 10, 2004, https://www.nytimes.com/2004/12/10/obituaries/nathan-most-is-dead-at-90-investment-fund-innovator.html.

7. "Global ETF Assets Soar Past $5trn Mark," TrackInsight, February 12, 2018, https://www.trackinsight.com/news/global-etf-assets-soar-past-5trn-mark/.

Bibliography

Balchunas, Eric. "Behind the ETF Revolution: How the US Government Inadvertently Launched an Industry." *Bloomberg Markets* 25, no. 1 (March 7, 2006).

Baldwin, Amy. "Vanguard, S&P in Licensing Tussle." MarketWatch, September 5, 2001. https://www.marketwatch.com/story/vanguard-sp-in-dispute-over-500-use-2001-09-05.

Bernstein, Peter L. *Capital Ideas: The Improbable Origins of Modern Wall Street*. Hoboken, NJ: Wiley, 2005.

Beutel, David. "William Fouse: The Greatest Investor You've Never Heard Of." Portfolio Strategy. Seeking Alpha, April 17, 2013. https://seekingalpha.com/article/1349101-william-fouse-the-greatest-investor-youve-never-heard-of?page=1.

Bruchey, Stuart. *The Modernization of the American Stock Exchange 1971–1989*. New York: Garland Publishing, 1991.

Carlson, Debbie. "Happy 25th Birthday: The SPY ETF Changed Investing." Funds. US News, January 18, 2018. https://money.usnews.com/investing/funds/articles/2018-01-18/happy-25th-birthday-the-spy-etf-changed-investing.

Carrel, Lawrence. *ETFs for the Long Run: What They Are, How They Work, and Simple Strategies for Successful Long-Term Investing*. Hoboken, NJ: Wiley, 2008.

Caskey, John P. "The Evolution of the Philadelphia Stock Exchange." *Federal Reserve Bank of Philadelphia Business Review* Q2 (2004): 18–29. https://www.philadelphiafed.org/-/media/research-and-data/publications/business-review/2004/q2/brq204jc2.pdf?la=en.

———. "The Evolution of the Philadelphia Stock Exchange: 1964–2002." Working Paper No. 03-21, Swarthmore College, Swarthmore, PA, 2003. https://www.philadelphiafed.org/-/media/research-and-data/publications/working-papers/2003/wp03-21.pdf.

Cboe. "Cboe History." http://www.cboe.com/aboutcboe/history.

Celtnet Telecommunications Companies. "The End of AT&T." Celtnet.org. Wayback Machine Internet Archive. https://web.archive.org/web/20090112213916/http://www.celtnet.org.uk:80/telecos/AT&T-Bell-4.php.

Chernoff, Joel. "Barclays Global Investors Boss Takes a Powder: What Next for the Index King?" *InvestmentNews*, July 20, 1998. https://www.investmentnews.com/article/19980720/SUB/807200714/barclays-global-investors-boss-takes-a-powder-what-next-for-the-Indexing-King.

Chow, K. Victor. "An Economic Interpretation of the ETF Revolution: Suggestions for China ETF Innovation." Working Paper, University of West Virginia, 2005. http://www.sse.com.cn/aboutus/research/workstation/c/station20050930.pdf.

Cision. "Toronto Stock Exchange Celebrates 20 Years of Listing and Trading Exchange-Traded Funds." News release. April 22, 2010. https://www.newswire.ca/news-releases/

toronto-stock-exchange-celebrates-20-years-of-listing-and-trading-exchangetraded-funds-539726331.html.

CME Group. "The Story of Futures Products." Stories of Financial Ingenuity and Innovation. 2018. http://www.cmegroup.com/stories/index.html#!4-products-land.

CME Group. "Timeline of CME Achievements." https://www.cmegroup.com/company/history/timeline-of-achievements.html.

CNBC. "Milestones of the Dow Industrials." US News. April 25, 2007. https://www.cnbc.com/id/18274839.

Costello, Martine. "Globetrotting with WEBS: World Equity Benchmark Shares (WEBS) Act Like Global Index Funds." Investing. CNN Money, June 10, 1998. https://money.cnn.com/1998/06/10/investing/q_webs/.

Crockett, Barton. "Wells, Nikko Selling Money Manager to Barcclays PLC." *American Banker*, June 22, 1995. https://www.americanbanker.com/news/wells-nikko-selling-money-manager-to-barcclays-plc.

Denmark, Frances. "Happy 20th Birthday, ETFs: A Look Back at Nate Most and His Novel Idea." Portfolio. *Institutional Investor*, July 3, 2013. https://www.institutionalinvestor.com/article/b14zb9jjc7wzv1/happy-20th-birthday-etfs-a-look-back-at-nate-most-and-his-novel-idea#Frances+Denmark.

ETF.com. "SPY ETF Report: SPDR S&P 500 ETF TrustRatings, Analysis, Quotes, Holdings." ETF.com. https://www.etf.com/SPY#overview.

Fabozzi, Frank, ed. *Handbook of Finance*. Vol. 1, *Financial Markets and Instruments*. New York: Wiley, 2008.

FINRA. "Flashback Wall Street: Black Monday." October 14, 2016. http://www.finra.org/investors/flashback-wall-street-black-monday.

FINRA. "NASD and AMEX Merger Completed: The NASDAQ-AMEX Market Group Formed." News release. November 2, 1998. http://www.finra.org/newsroom/1998/nasd-and-amex-merger-completed-nasdaq-amex-market-group-formed.

FINRA. "When Paper Paralyzed Wall Street: Remembering the 1960s Paperwork Crisis." August 19, 2015. https://www.finra.org/investors/when-paper-paralyzed-wall-street-remembering-1960s-paperwork-crisis.

Fuhr, Deborah. "ETFs Are Busting Out All Over." ETF.com. January 1, 2001. https://www.etf.com/publications/journalofindexes/joi-articles/1251.html.

Gastineau, Gary L. *The Exchange-Traded Funds Manual*. New York: Wiley, 2002.

Groves, Megan. "The Birth of the Modern Stock Market." Cincinnati Stock Exchange. http://www.cincinnatistockexchange.us/the-birth-of-the-modern-stock-market-automation-and-impact/.

Grundfest, Joseph A. "'Perestroika' on Wall Street: The Future of Securities Trading." Speech presented at the Financial Executives Institute's 57th Annual Conference, San Francisco, CA, October 12, 1988. SEC.gov, https://www.sec.gov/news/speech/1988/101288grundfest.pdf.

Hakansson, Nils H. "The Purchasing Power Fund: A New Kind of Financial Intermediary." *Financial Analysts Journal* 32, no. 6 (November–December 1976): 49–59.

Hill, Edwin C. "The Strangest Stock Market in the World: The Curb Market on Broad Street, a Unique New York Institution Which Is an Extraordinary Spectacle as Well as a Highly Important Financial Center." *Munsey's Magazine* 69 (February–May 1920): 46, https://books.google.com/books?id=BKPNAAAAMAAJ.

Investment Company Institute. "US Closed-End Funds." In *2018 Investment Company Fact Book: A Review of Trends and Activities in the Investment Company Industry.* http://www.icifactbook. org/ch5/18_fb_ch5.

Investopedia. "Best Time(s) of Day, Week & Month to Trade Stocks." Trading Strategy. Updated October 29, 2018. https://www.investopedia.com/day-trading/ best-time-day-week-month-trade-stocks/.

Jarrow, Robert A., and Maureen O'Hara. "Primes and Scores: An Essay on Market Imperfections." *Journal of Finance* 55, iss. 5 (December 1989): 1264. Wiley Online Library. https:// onlinelibrary.wiley.com/doi/abs/10.1111/j.1540-6261.1989. tb02653.x.

Kharouf, Jim. "Ivers Riley: A Man for All Markets." John Lothian News. February 18, 2015. http://johnlothiannews.com/ ivers-riley-man-markets/.

Klitgaard, Thomas, and James Narron. "Crisis Chronicles: The Long Depression and the Panic of 1873." *Liberty Street Economics* (blog). Federal Reserve Bank of New York, February 5, 2016. https://libertystreeteconomics.newyorkfed.org/2016/02/

crisis-chronicles-the-long-depression-and-the-panic-of-1873.html.

Kupfer, Andrew. "Leland, O'Brien, and Rubinstein: The Guys Who Gave Us Portfolio Insurance." *Fortune*, January 4, 1988. http://archive.fortune.com/magazines/fortune/fortune_archive/1988/01/04/70047/index.htm.

Ludwig, Olivier. "Bogle: ETF Trading Has No Social Value." ETF.com. September 29, 2011. https://www.etf.com/sections/features/9947-bogle-etf-trading-has-no-social-value.html.

Lybecker, Martin E. "Bank-Sponsored Investment Management Services: Consideration of the Regulation Problems, and Suggested Legislative and Statutory Interpretive Responses." *Duke Law Journal* 1977, no. 5 (December 1977): 983.

Maiello, Michael. "2005 Mutual Fund Survey: The Un-Vanguard." *Forbes*, September 19, 2005. https://www.forbes.com/free_forbes/2005/0919/182.html.

Markowitz, Harry. "Portfolio Selection." *Journal of Finance* 7, no. 1 (March 1952): 77–91.

Mayer, Martin. "Suddenly, It's Chicago." *New York Times Magazine*, March 27, 1988. https://www.nytimes.com/1988/03/27/magazine/suddenly-it-s-chicago.html.

Mendes, Joshua, and Andrew Evan Serwer. "This Exxon Stock Comes Custom-Blended." *Fortune*, May 12, 1986. http://archive.fortune.com/magazines/fortune/fortune_archive/1986/05/12/67526/index.htm.

Owens, Hugh F. "The SEC and Securities Markets—Some Current Developments." Address presented at the Texas

Group Investment Bankers Association of America, Dallas, TX, April 7, 1966. SEC.gov. https://www.sec.gov/news/speech/1966/040766owens.pdf.

Reuters. "Nasdaq to Pay $140 Million for Amex Merger." Business. *Wired*, March 18, 1998. https://www.wired.com/1998/03/nasdaq-to-pay-140-million-for-amex-merger/.

Riley, Ivers. "ETF: The 'Hail Mary' Security." *Modern Trader* 34, no. 4 (March 2006). Questia. https://www.questia.com/magazine/1P3-995467691/etf-the-hail-mary-security.

Roy, Sumit. "2017 ETF Inflows Big Record Breaker." ETF.com. Updated January 2, 2018. https://www.etf.com/sections/weekly-etf-flows/2017-etf-inflows-big-record-breaker.

Russo, Thomas A., and Edwin Lyon. "The Exclusive Jurisdiction of the Commodity Futures Trading Commission." *Hofstra Law Review* 6, iss. 1 (1977): 57–91. Scholarly Commons at Hofstra Law. https://scholarlycommons.law.hofstra.edu/cgi/viewcontent.cgi?article=1196&context=hlr.

Securities and Exchange Commission Historical Society. "In the Midst of Revolution: The SEC, 1973–1981." http://www.sechistorical.org/museum/galleries/rev/rev02c.php.

Sobel, Robert. *The Curbstone Brokers: The Origins of the American Stock Exchange*. New York: Macmillan, 1970.

State Street Global Advisors. *SPDR S&P 500 ETF Trust: A Unit Investment Trust*. September 30, 2018. https://us.spdrs.com/public/SPDR%20SP%20500%20ETF%209.30.18%20Web%20Ready.pdf.

———. "SPY: The Idea That Spawned an Industry." SEC.gov,

January 25, 2013. https://www.sec.gov/Archives/edgar/data/1222333/000119312513023294/d473476dfwp.htm.

Statista. "Total Net Assets of US-Registered Mutual Funds Worldwide from 1998 to 2017 (in Trillion U.S. Dollars)." 2018. https://www.statista.com/statistics/255518/mutual-fund-assets-held-by-investment-companies-in-the-united-states/.

TrackInsight. "Global ETF Assets Soar Past $5trn Mark." February 12, 2018. https://www.trackinsight.com/news/global-etf-assets-soar-past-5trn-mark/.

Tufano, Peter, and Barbara B. Kyrillos. "Leland O'Brien Rubinstein Associates, Inc.: SuperTrust." Case Study. *Harvard Business Review* (June 6, 1994).

Twomey, Brian. "The International Money Market." Managing Wealth. Investopedia. Updated January 20, 2010. https://www.investopedia.com/articles/forex/10/international-money-market.asp.

US Commodity Futures Trading Commission. "CFTC History in the 1980s." https://www.cftc.gov/About/HistoryoftheCFTC/history_1980s.html.

US Department of the Treasury. *Report of the Presidential Task Force on Market Mechanisms: Submitted to the President of the United States, the Secretary of the Treasury, and the Chairman of the Federal Reserve Board.* Washington, DC: US Department of the Treasury, 1988.

US Securities and Exchange Commission. *The October 1987 Market Break: A Report by the Division of Market Regulation US Securities and Exchange Commission.* Washington, DC: Securities and

Exchange Commission, 1988. https://babel.hathitrust.org/cgi/pt?id=mdp.35128000946994;view=1up;seq=1.

Vitiello, Dominic, with George E. Thomas. *The Philadelphia Stock Exchange and the City It Made.* Philadelphia: University of Pennsylvania Press, 2010.

Wells Fargo. "Stagecoach History." Wells Fargo History. https://www.wellsfargohistory.com/history/.

Wiandt, Jim. "Nate Most, Exchange-Traded Fund Inventor, Dies at Age 90." ETF.com. December 8, 2004. https://www.etf.com/sections/features/281.html?nopaging=1.

———. "S&P Prevails—Vanguard Loses Landmark Lawsuit." Index Fund Advisors. April 26, 2001, https://www.ifa.com/articles/SP_PrevailsVanguard_Loses_Landmark_Lawsuit/.

Wikipedia. "Pecora Commission." Updated September 5, 2018. https://en.wikipedia.org/wiki/Pecora_Commission.

RALPH LEHMAN, CFA, CAIA, JD/MBA, has spent twenty years managing portfolios for clients and advising them on investment, tax, estate, and financial planning issues. When he first encountered ETFs, he was intrigued by the hybrid security that was changing how people could invest in the markets. He began researching the ETF's history and noticed that no one had written a full account of the incredible story of these funds. What began as a hobby of ordinary research and several curious phone calls progressed into writing a book about how the first ETFs were developed.

Ralph is currently an investment advisor in the retirement industry, working with both defined benefit and defined contribution plans. Prior to his career in finance, he spent nine years mentoring and training college students in a discipleship-focused ministry while spending his summers working with youth in inner-city ministry.

When Ralph is not attempting to tame his unruly yard, he enjoys jogging and swimming. He is an avid reader and studies a broad range of subjects—including classical, Church, US, and world history; finance; economics; and law. Ralph and his wife, Charlotte, live in Knoxville, Tennessee, with their Brittany, Rocky.

Lightning Source UK Ltd.
Milton Keynes UK
UKHW020740140922
408851UK00009B/912

9 781612 543406